MW00487560

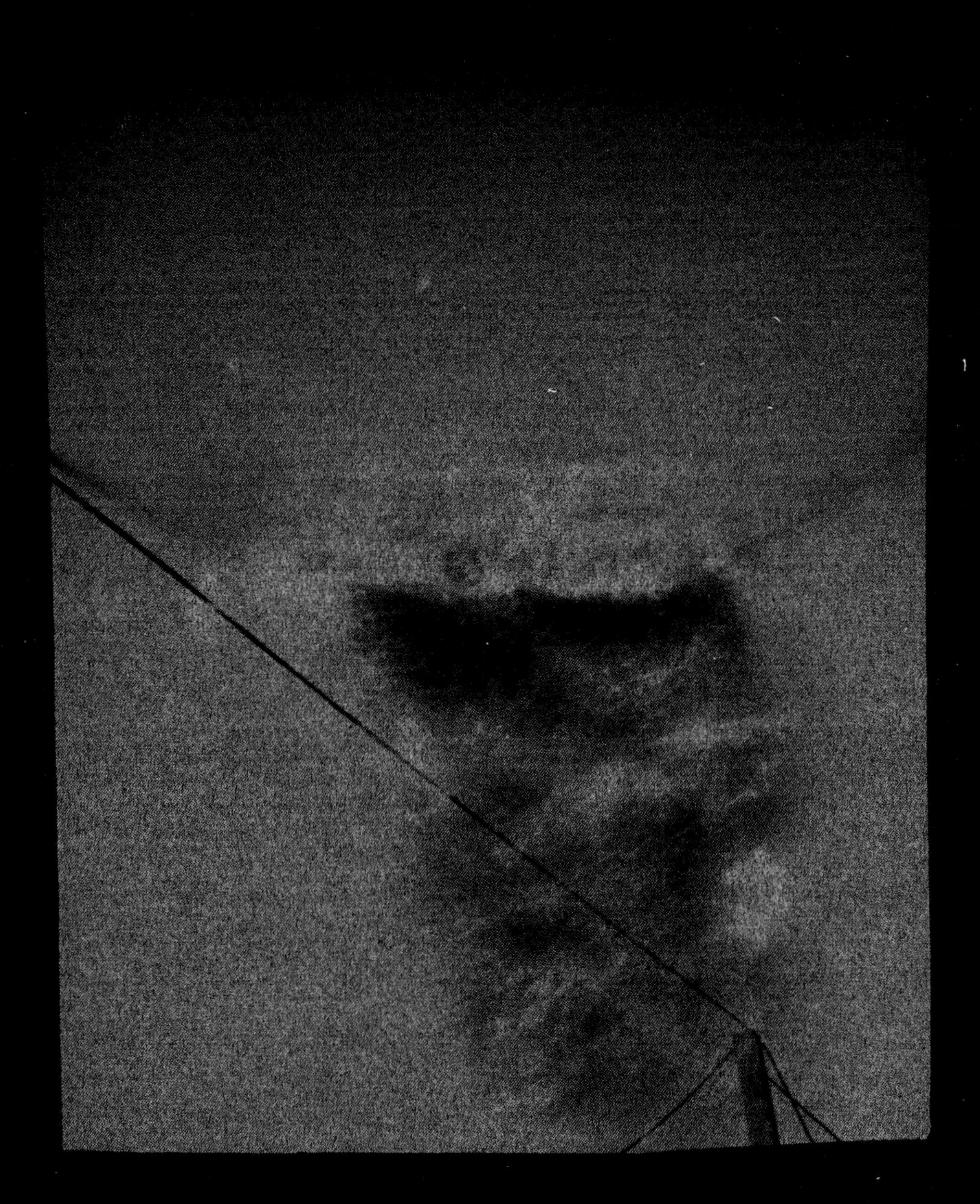

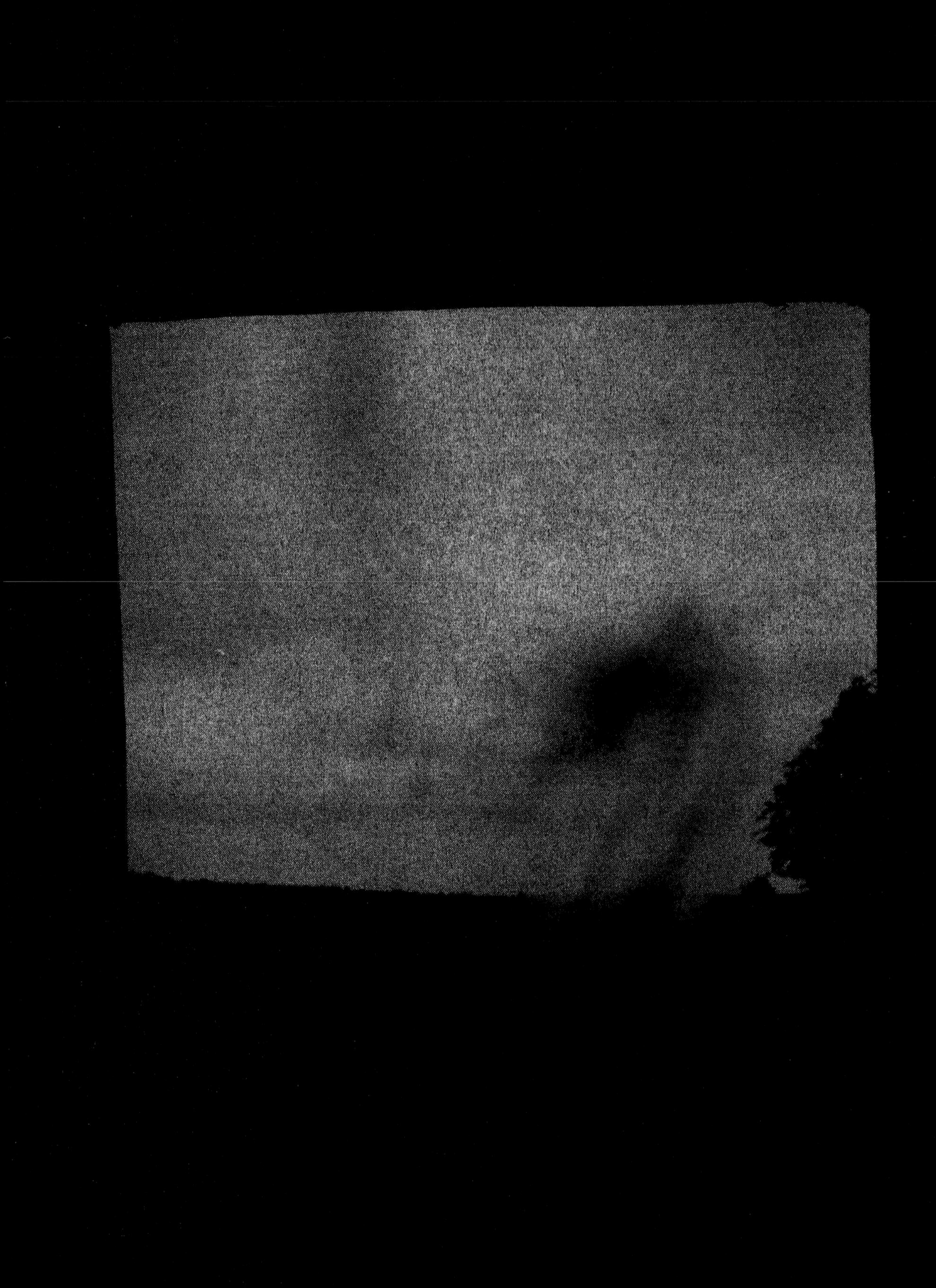

Harold Mendez: The years now

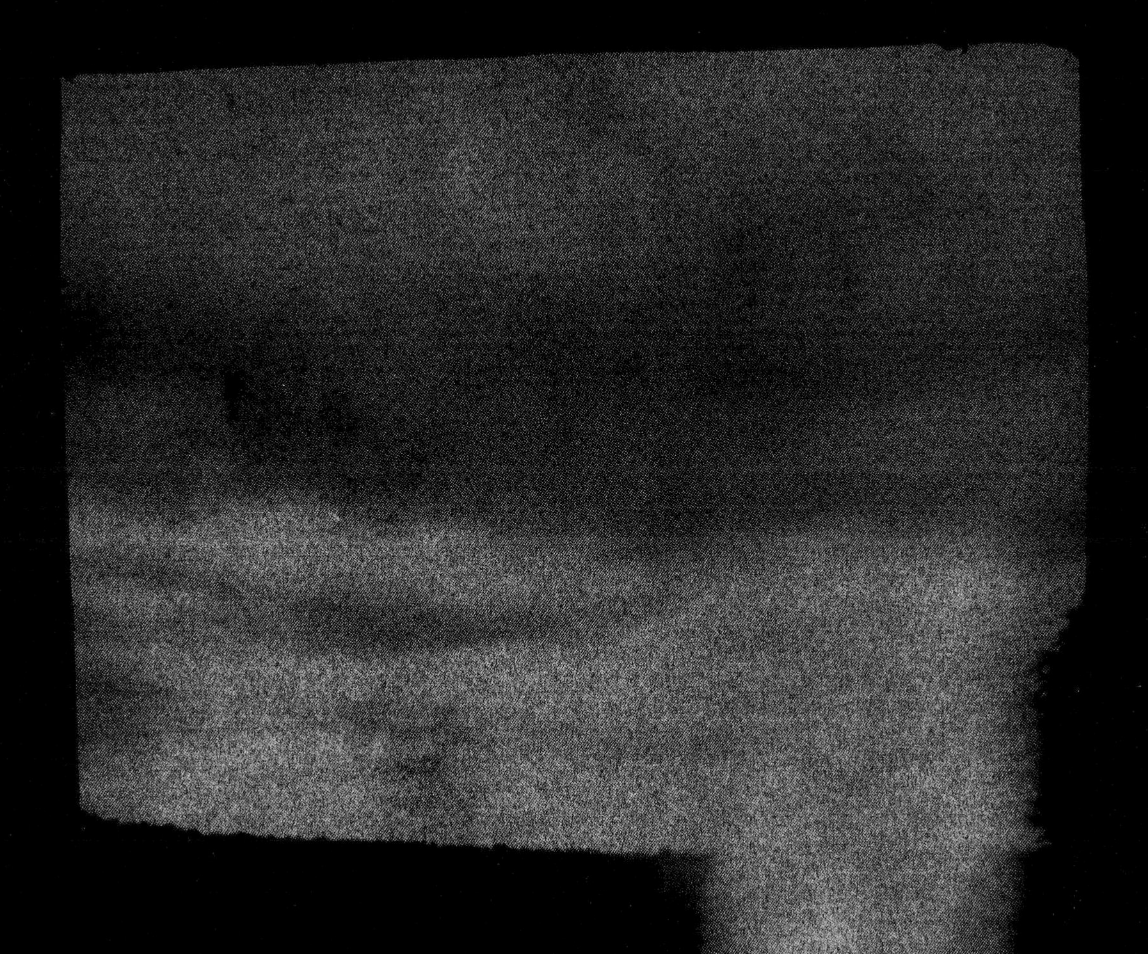

Edited by
Yesomi Umolu

Reva and David Logan Center
for the Arts at the University of Chicago

CONTENTS

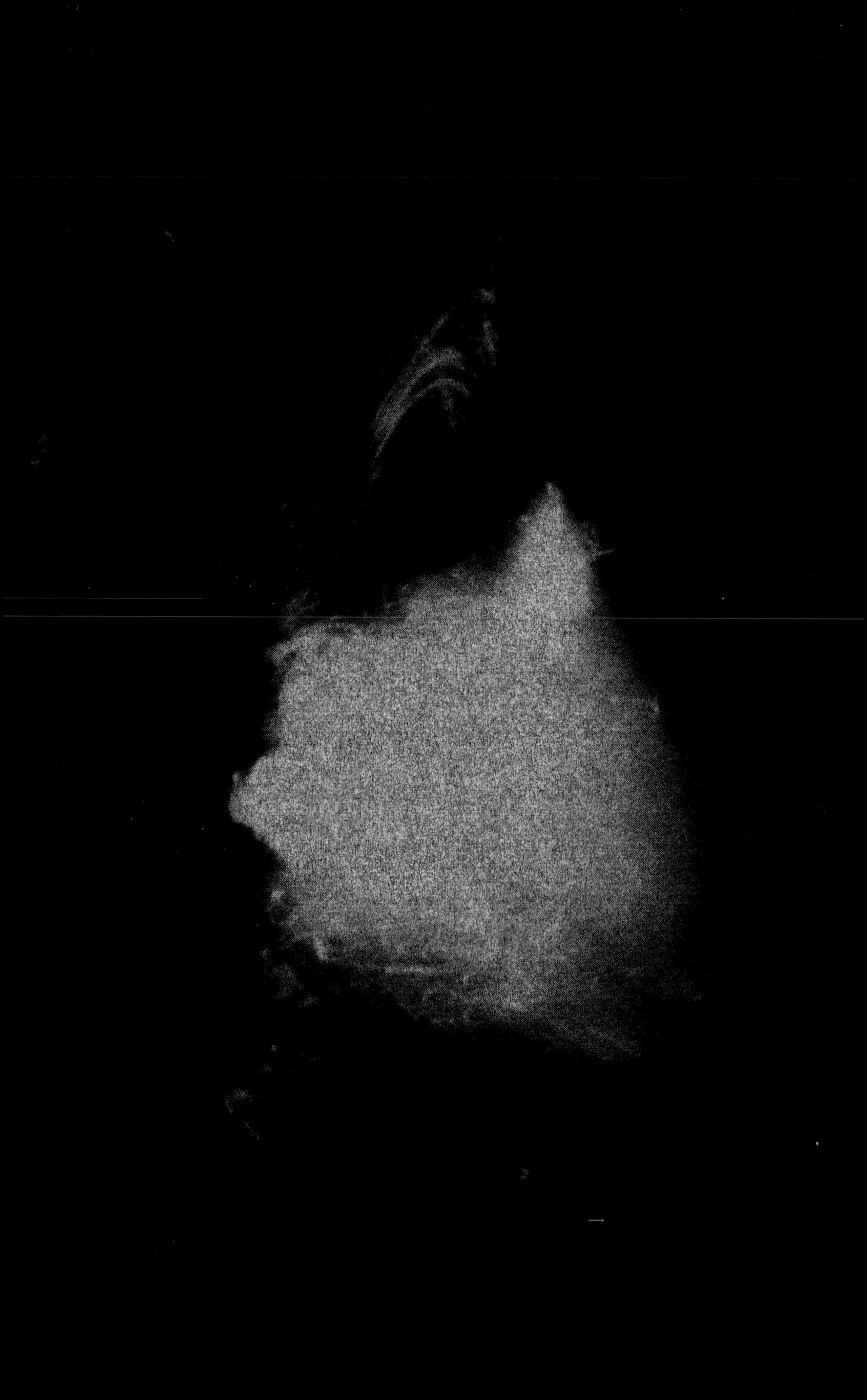

FOREWORD

Published in conjunction with *Harold Mendez: The years now*, an exhibition presented in 2020 at the Reva and David Logan Center for the Arts at the University of Chicago, this volume unpacks the Los Angeles-based artist's deft weaving of multiple narratives with symbolic materials and found objects. At the heart of Mendez's practice is a fascination with unearthing the complex story of the Americas, spanning from ancient times through the colonial era and into the present day. His exhibition at the Logan Center Gallery showcased new and existing photographic, sound, and sculptural works that explore the body's connections to acts of violence and erasure, on the one hand, and renewal and remembrance on the other. Skillfully and thoughtfully arranged, these elements came together to highlight the ways in which conceptions of the self are deeply connected to divergent histories and geographies.

The exhibition was realized in close collaboration with curatorial lead Katja Rivera, former Assistant Curator; Alyssa Brubaker, Exhibitions Manager; Marcus Warren, Shop and Gallery Manager; and Peter Reese, Assistant Director of Logan Shops. We thank the Logan Center Exhibitions team for their expertise, patience, and care throughout the development of this project. We are grateful to the students at the University of Chicago who assisted with the installation: Tony Auth, Martin Girardi, and Isaac Rand. We also extend our thanks to the staff of the Jonathan Logan Family Foundation Media Center, particularly David Wolf, Senior Director of Arts Technologies; Ben Chandler, Assistant Director; Will Cabaniss, Media Center Coordinator; and Justin Williams, former Training and Community Manager, who provided technical assistance for the show. And we acknowledge the Communications office: Ronia Holmes, Director of Communications, and Clare Austen-Smith, Digital Content Manager. Special thanks are due to Stacey Recht, Director of Development, and her staff. For their guidance and help with the logistical details of this project, we thank Greg Redenius, Director for Facilities and Operations, and his colleagues. We are also immensely grateful to Alex Inglizian, Technical Director and Chief Engineer at Experimental Sound Studio in Chicago, for his enthusiasm in working with the artist to realize his multichannel sound installation. Special thanks to the Anthropology department at the Field Museum, Chicago, especially JP Brown, Regenstein Conservator for Pacific Anthropology; Lauren Hancock, Registrar; and Ryan Williams, Associate Curator and Section Head, for their expertise and consultation on the ancient artifacts in their collection. Thanks are also due to Sara Kelly at the School of the Art Institute of Chicago for facilitating 3-D printing of objects in the exhibition.

The years now was made possible through the lead support of the David C. and Sarajean Ruttenberg Arts Foundation, with additional funding provided by the Reva and David Logan Foundation, the Revada Foundation, and friends of the Logan Center. We are grateful to the David C. and Sarajean Ruttenberg Arts Foundation and PATRON Gallery, Chicago, for their support of this publication.

As Mendez's first monograph, this publication was developed with the intent of elucidating the artist's practice beyond the confines of his project at the Logan Center. Across these pages, readers are enveloped in his daily explorations of place, materials, and sculptural form. We would like to thank the contributing writers, Candice Hopkins and J. Michael Martinez, for their singular and provocative readings of the artist's work, and Katja Rivera for her illuminating conversation with the artist. This publication's design has benefited from the ingenuity and intuition of Marco Balesteros of Letra. We are also grateful to Amanda Glesmann for her editorial precision and to Alyssa Brubaker for her skill as publication manager.

Above all, we are proud to have realized this project with Harold, whom we thank for accepting our invitation with great enthusiasm. The Logan Center prides itself on being an institution that wholeheartedly supports artists in their endeavors, providing space for big ideas to be realized in close collaboration with our talented team, our faculty and students, and the cultural community across Chicago. Our work is infinitely enriched by the creativity and experimentation of artists such as Harold, who continue to redefine the boundaries of contemporary practice in ever more eloquent and decisive ways.

Bill Michel, Associate Provost and Executive Director,
UChicago Arts and the Reva and David Logan Center for the Arts

Yesomi Umolu, Director and Curator, Logan Center Exhibitions

Entanglements Are Also about Life and Death

Candice
Hopkins

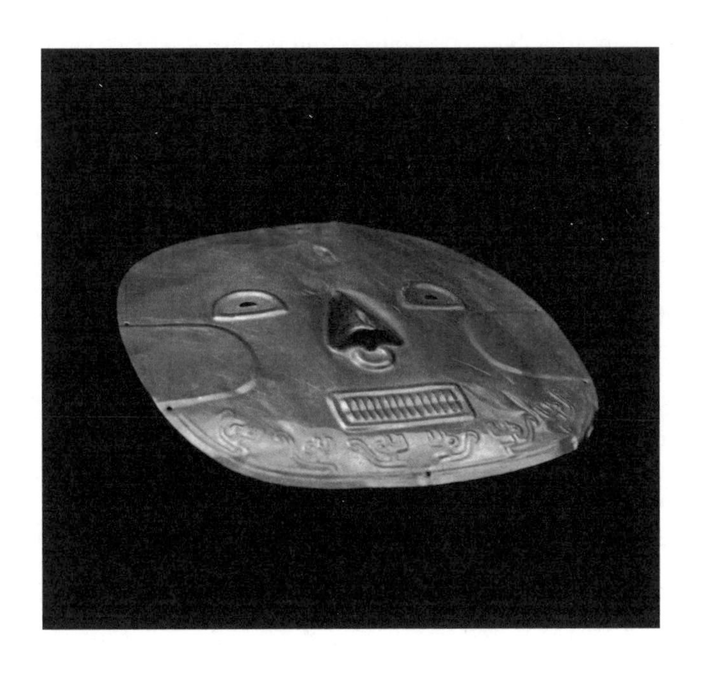

The arms of a small clay monkey grasp the neck of a pre-Incan vessel–or rather the digital replica of such a vessel, one rubbed dark with graphite. Out of its neck comes a recorded voice. A man's words rise and fall, sentences and their fragments moving around the room through an array of speakers, at times booming and at other moments silent. A seed pod with part of its outer shell peeled away forms the vessel's body. Its slender ends curl upward like a mouth, complete with seeds as teeth. Yet the pot is not the only one smiling; the monkey also grins.

(I am thinking of the gallery as a vessel.)
(I am thinking about entanglements.)

The pot is small but it called to me first. Something in its digital presence calls to the original too. This original, made by Chimú people, is not an artifact–spelled variously with an *e* or an *i*–but a cultural belonging. Museums, with their lingering primitivist ideologies and tendencies toward salvage anthropology, have tried with little success to rid these belongings of their agency, first by separating them from their people. Seeing the pot now is a reminder that its true home is elsewhere, with others. Its lifecycle has been interrupted; it lives now in a permanent stasis, the non-life of the cultural object. Museums suspend death and decay while simultaneously defending their bounty from the living (organisms, insects, rot, and humans alike).

The pots, the masks, the regalia, the spiritual items, the implements for healing and transformation–they all come from particular places and were made by someone for another. Now displaced, they did not ask to be tucked away on metal shelves, in boxes or under wraps along with thousands of their kin. They did not ask to be put on display and gazed at with uninitiated eyes, to be opened up and their contents revealed, photographed, sold, or discarded. Made by ancient brown hands, this vessel was imbued with life before it was released into the world. The recorded voice emanates out of it now, like breath. With each spoken word the seed-pod smile grows wider.

Joaquiniquil, cuaniquil, guama, guaba, *Inga edulis,* ice cream bean. The sweet, white pulp of the pod tastes like vanilla with hints of cinnamon. When cooked, its tough black seeds are rich and dense, like chickpeas. And when the rains begin, birds and monkeys flock to the trees to feast on the pods, their cries signaling to others that the bounty is ready to eat. In their excitement they scatter the seeds, which sprout when the conditions are right. The pods also have medicinal properties. They aid with rheumatism and can calm the bowels, and for millennia people have made drinks from seeds that have been chewed by women and spit into a pot, where they are left to ferment. Perhaps this vessel didn't contain the seeds but rather held the drink, a drink that can bring about shifts in consciousness as well as exaltation. This is how the ceremonialists transit between worlds. The pot is not decorative or simply "utilitarian" (there's no need to abide by the patronizing discourse of craft here), rather its conceptual design signals all of these uses, from the practical to the spiritual, signaled first by its perpetual smile.

(I am thinking of alchemy.)
(I am thinking about proximity.)

Moving from the wall-mounted vessel and tracing the circumference of the first gallery space, you simultaneously trace the perimeter of a low-lying fiberglass grid. The grid's size and shape create a contemplative choreography with the viewer and the objects. A charred root or a tangle of thick branches rests near the middle of the structure, as if emerging from the grid like a weed. Delicate, creamy petals are scattered among the grid's small squares, some already dried and creased while others appear to have fallen yesterday from a tree that's since disappeared. The petals cause something of a temporal rupture: although the root is weathered and aged, the petals have yet to decay and remain tethered to their prior being.

There is a generative proximity between the graphite-rubbed root (charcoal embodying the material transformation of wood burned down to carbon) and the fiberglass plane that glints silver and gold. Is there tentative comfort in the intimacy of disparate forms? The visible fragments simultaneously draw attention to what is not there: the rough-hewn trunk gestures to a missing tree that like a phantom limb is acutely felt but not seen, while petals signal to absent flowers and the grid stands in for an entire city. These entanglements are also about life and death, as is their relative proximity, particularly in this age of a pandemic crisis.[1]

In the adjacent gallery, the trunk of another tree is suspended in the center of a steel pole, which itself appears to grow from the corner of a chalky white wall. Looking closely reveals the moment when the fence and the tree became one: the sharp ends of cut chain-link protrude from the very heart of the tree's trunk. Did this enfolding lead to its death, or was the tree cut down because it interfered with the fence? We have an obsessive tendency to put up barriers, to guard artificial boundaries and property, to stake our claims. But fences are permeable, themselves victim to growth and change.

This attentive gathering of objects produces a constellation of narratives that fold and unfold, build up and fall away. This is a conscious interpellation: it is what the artist describes as a one-act play. What is revealed by the productive oscillation between what is there and not there, between the remains and the whole? Can these shards stand in for broader histories?

From a distance an adjacent photograph gives the impression that the artist hung a piece of stone directly on the wall. The picture is itself evidence of geologic or deep time. Fossilized coral is visible along its edges, while a single brown feather–from a bird's tail or its wing–rests in a cavity along the bottom right. I wonder whether the feather was lost when the bird flew overhead, or if it was placed there as part of a ritual? In the center, concentric circles of red, yellow, and blue pigment appear like a portal, framing the place of belief. We know that ritual is a way to heal, to make connections, to be in relation with the living and the dead. What ceremony took place here? What was conjured? What connections were made?

> *(Pay attention to the traces.)*
> *(Pay attention to the traces.)*

I am thinking about the things made visible–the vessel, the roots, the trunks, the grids, the petals, the feather, the portal, the pole, the sound–as well as those made present through their absence. I am thinking about how they are in relation to one another and how the viewer is in relation to them, as a witness. In Mendez's collection of things, all found and carefully repurposed, I find the specters of history. We are haunted by unrequited pasts and the inevitable return of former traumas, particularly those that are buried away, covered over and deliberately forgotten. The Americas are founded on this amnesia, the deliberate forgetting and active suppression of the violence of their origins. This violence didn't take place all at once, but over hundreds of years, unfolding like a slow genocide.[2]

This continues today and is not limited to people, but extends to our environments as well. While the replica of the Chumi vessel cannot (and should not) stand in for these histories, it nonetheless draws attention to the specters of the past.

Paying attention to the vessel (which set everything in motion) and the recorded voice is a reminder that voice is the only constant in the exhibition; that is, it is the only thing that occupies all of the rooms even in its silence. In Mendez's work it is these silences that are made full and ever present.

(From silences to soundings)
(Closing our eyes and opening our ears)

In 1953 the late Pauline Oliveros listened to a tape recording that captured the sounds outside her apartment window. I imagine that they were a mix of nature–the rustling of leaves, or the chirp of a common sparrow and the low rumble of a car engine, its rubber tires undulating against the pavement. What the composer learned upon playing back the recording was that despite having listened, she hadn't *heard* everything in that short period of time. She later dedicated her practice to dismantling sonic hierarchies, following her own advice: "Listen to everything all the time and remind yourself when you are not listening."[3] In Mendez's installation, recorded sound moves around the rooms in ebbs and flows, never playing the same loop. The original found recording has been subtly altered with layers of additional sound and programmed so that new compositions are infinitely arranged. While certain words and sentences repeat themselves, they are never heard in the same way. Mendez describes the recording as representing an existential crisis in speech, complete with its own gaps and instances of (sonic) intelligibility.[4]

Repeating sounds, overlapping sounds. A ceremony of sound. To break the spell or the convention of time that we adhere to. Music is the basis for every ceremony, just as art is the basis for every ritual. Like recorded sound, copies enables us to see the originals differently. Is there comfort in unknown origins, in endings rather than beginnings? Mendez is always making new copies–even of sound recordings–to the point that any penchant for the authenticity of the original falls away. Mendez's gesture of repatriation is not focused on an object's return as a historical corrective (however needed), but on its recapitulation through the invention of new dwellings, of new worlds for the copies.

Museums are doing this as well, but differently. Not willing to let go of their hoards, at least not entirely, they too are making copies. They are producing exacting prints of things like ceremonial masks by first photographing every aspect of them, including their insides. Printed in plastic are eyes carved by hand, articulating wooden beaks, ornately designed cheekbones (both bird and human), feathers, even the mask's imperfections are replicated. Then they are regifting these ersatz ceremonial masks back to the community so that local artists can "complete" them based on a mix of customary and invented protocols. They are painting them as though they are made of wood, they are adding leather ties to them, they are affixing feathers and other items. They are then dancing these new masks in abridged ceremonies that take place inside the museums. The newly authenticated copy has truly come home. And instead of giving the original masks back to the community, museums are gifting them the copies instead.

These are new copies for new times.

It's worth remembering that the museum (like the gallery) is a frame, but not a conventional one–its edges can shift; it creates borders within borders, which can act as dividing lines between us and them, particularly when it comes to questions of ownership, rights, and the rehoming of our belongings. When conversations first began with museums regarding the return of our ancestors' bones, as well as those things that were outright stolen or sold under duress, this frame was used as the basis to refuse their return. Once they enter museums these objects become bound by museological protocols, protocols that they then carry with them when they are eventually returned to their places of origin. To some they appear homesick even in their return–stuck between worlds.

Given this pandemic age, it's worth reiterating that one of the reasons museums give for not returning our things is that they have been poisoned–sickened by the institution's treatment in the early days of collecting, when it was routine to douse these objects with arsenic as they entered their holdings. This was a true performance of fearing contamination by the Other, yet wanting these things nonetheless. Our things can't come home because they are now toxic. Another more complex narrative of refusal furthers this rhetoric of sickness and infection–the idea that cultural belongings may carry with them very old diseases to which Indigenous communities no longer have immunities. *If they return they will make us sick.* Colonial infection has come to be wielded as an excuse to keep from us those things that are rightfully ours.

Yet, as Mendez's installation reminds us, these are things with agency. Mendez mobilizes other ways of being with them, of making them a part of us, of our bodies. Is this a part of the restoration and repair? He extends this conversation beyond those things made and emitted by us to include other beings–the trees, the scattering of petals, the traces of birds–that have intervened in our inventions, particularly those that have served to distance us from nature.

Mendez has created a ritual of things and in doing so reminded us that rituals are also about healing.

Pay attention to the traces, to the shards that stand in for history.

NOTES

1. This essay was written during the months of March and April 2020, when the virus COVID-19 was declared a pandemic, thus having spread to nearly every part of the globe and radically changed daily life, causing severe economic downturns and mass job losses in many nations, and overrunning health-care systems worldwide, including in Europe and the Americas. At the time of this writing, there were upward of 38.7 million documented cases worldwide and more than one million deaths.

2. It's worth restating that 90% of the estimated 60 to 112 million people who prior to colonization lived in what are now the Americas were victim to waves of conquest, colonialism, and disease.

3. Pauline Oliveros, quoted in Seán Street, *Sound Poetics: Interaction and Personal Identity* (Cham, Switzerland: Palgrave Macmillan, 2017), 110.

4. In correspondence with the author in February 2020, Harold Mendez provided a transcription of the found audio file, which is reprinted on page 67 of this volume.

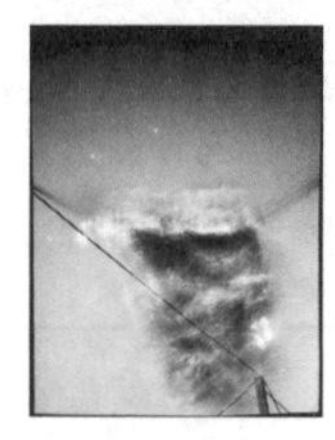

If we bring our specters into the open, it may save us from disaster, 2013–14. Digital print transferred from unique pinhole photograph. Collection of Harry and Ellen Parker

At night we walk in circles, n.d. Lantern slide

Study for *Nobody / Braille Teeth*, 2013–14. Resin-coated photo paper

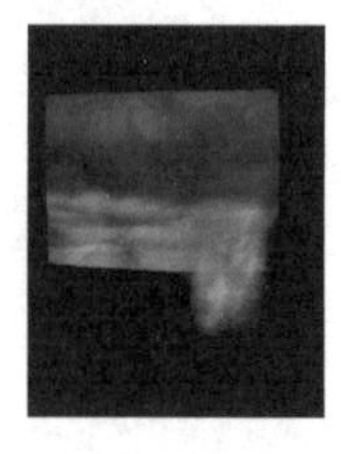

Untitled (Skowhegan), 2013. Resin-coated photo paper

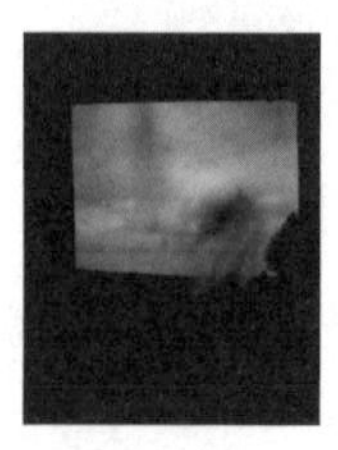

Untitled (Skowhegan), 2013. Resin-coated photo paper

Untitled, 2013–14. Resin-coated photo paper

Olmec mask, n.d. The Metropolitan Museum of Art, New York, bequest of Alice K. Bache, 1977

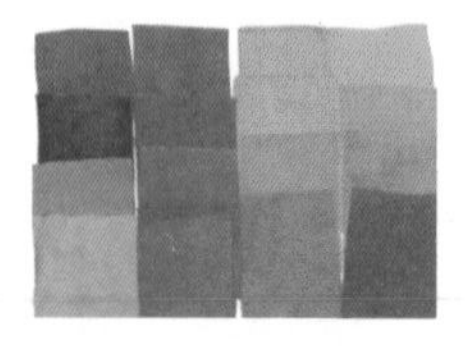

Dye silk samples made with madder and cochineal, using various mordant and dyebath modifications, 1992. Produced by Elena Phipps, © Elena Phipps

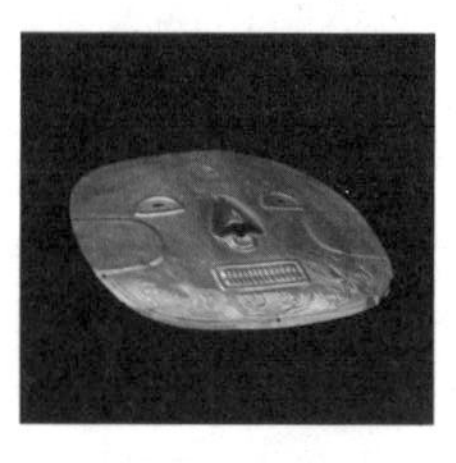

Orfebrería precolombina (pre-Columbian goldwork), n.d., Museo del Oro, Bogotá. Biblioteca Pública Piloto de Medellín para América Latina

Chimú pot, n.d. The Field Museum, Image No. CL0048_170032_FrontAngle, Cat. No 170032. Photo: Sarah Rivers, © The Field Museum

Still from the making of *when the night is going wrong or when the day is full of empty promise,* 2017. Collaboration with Tiffany & Co. for the 2017 Whitney Biennial, Whitney Museum of American Art, New York, 2017

Study for I'm not always fitting (After Koudelka), 2018. Gesso, toner and graphite on ball-grained lithographic plate

It is important, when transplanting plants, that their roots not be exposed to the air longer than is necessary. Failure to observe this caution will result in the plant dying eventually, if not immediately. When transplanting, you may notice a gently ripping sound as the roots are torn away from the soil. This is to be expected: for the plant, transplanting is always a painful process.

The Practical Guide to Gardening

Excerpt from *She Tries Her Tongue, Her Silence Softly Breaks* by M. NourbeSe Philip (1989)

I

but I sound better since you cut my throat, 2017.
Reclaimed galvanized steel, wood, and chain link fence

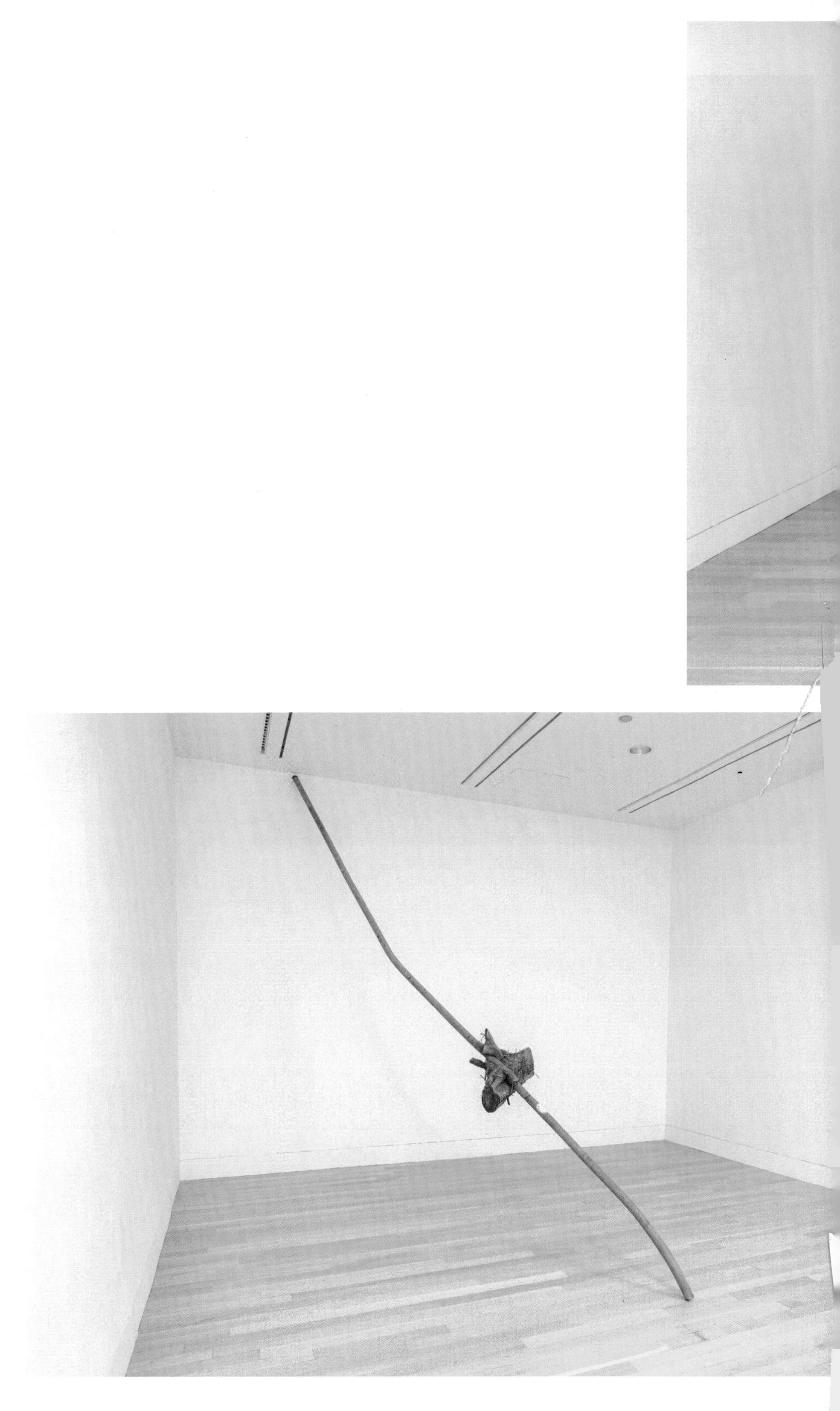

HAROLD MENDEZ

21

THE YEARS NOW

HAROLD MENDEZ

Harold Mendez in Conversation with Katja Rivera

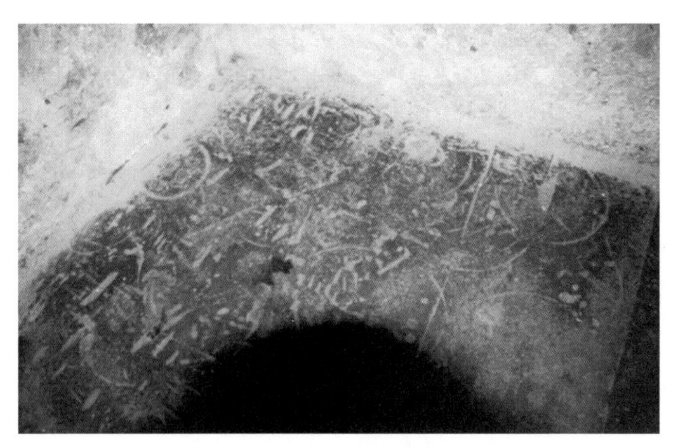

This text was excerpted from a recording made on March 14, 2020.

Katja Rivera: One of the works in *The years now* is an immersive multichannel sound installation that can only be experienced to its fullest extent with the appropriate surround-sound system. How did you choose the content and why did you decide to move the sound around the gallery the way that you did?

Harold Mendez: The sound installation consists of an unidentified person speaking about his life, asking himself questions about who he is. The exhibition's title is taken from a fragment of his speech, which is from a found recording (see p. 67). The speaker is talking about the very beginnings of life being painful, and assessing who he is–and I think that is a very existential thing to be asking yourself. I came across the recording while listening to an online radio show hosted by the founder of Standing on the Corner, an amorphous music collective from New York. The speech emerged at the tail end of the show. The vocals initially sound warped, like they were either played backward or were being delayed manually on a record player. And then there's this moment of clarity in the speech, which is immediately overlaid with a cacophonous sample of piano playing. The voice and the content of the speech are what really resonated with me. So much so that I would return to it while in the studio and play that fragment over and over. That continued off and on for about two years. During that time I tried finding out more about the speech: I wanted to know who was speaking, what was its context, and what the rest of the speech entailed, etc. Having no luck with traditional research methods, I shared it with a few people, like Fred Moten, Jamal Cyrus, and Hamza Walker, who I knew had a deep knowledge of music as well as text-based materials, and who I thought could help me identify the voice. To no avail. But later on, when I began to conceptualize work for this exhibition, I went back to that speech.

When I was much younger, I would go down to Maxwell Street, an open-air market in Chicago where you would hear music and recorded speeches by people like Malcolm X being played. I still have cassette tapes of some of those speeches. And then years later, when I lived in Houston's Third Ward, there was a Black Panther who would set up these large speakers outside on weekends, at the park next to the Eldorado Ballroom, and play these speeches by Malcolm X. I've always been really aware of Malcolm X and his politics, but hearing his voice–it's incredibly strong, it's powerful. And so just having those different experiences of listening to sound or a voice fill up a space made me think a lot about how a voice can carry a message.

KR: Can you speak a little more about your process as you were producing and installing the sound installation?

HM: I knew I wanted the voice to occupy the space in a similar way in the exhibition. Alex Inglizian from Experimental Sound Studio really helped me shape the sound and expand its possibilities.

You hear the sound first when you're walking into the gallery and then you encounter a field from which a tree-like sculpture emerges. I wanted the voice to really fill the space in ways that were sometimes very clear and articulate, to have the space at times engulfed in sound and then at other times to be very quiet. The playback of the piece is generative, with custom software making algorithmic decisions based on a set of rules that determine sonic localization, filtering, effect processing, playback position, and silence. An example of this is when the word "dangling" plays–the software grabs that word and diffuses it throughout the entire gallery on a select number of speakers so that it echoes and delays around the field and throughout the space. The installation includes many filters and effects such as this, each one having a different interaction with the original recording. Although the primary recording lasts only about two minutes, the way in which the software processes means it is never the same, and the listener's experience is continually changing. The sound was difficult to figure out. How to think about it sculpturally so that it resonates, not just for me but also for others who are listening to it or engaging with it as they're moving around.

KR: White carnation petals cover your central floor sculpture in *The years now,* and they were continuously replenished throughout the exhibition. You've also used carnation petals in previous sculptures. Can you address the use and reuse of this particular material in your practice?

HM: The petals first started with a sculpture that I made in 2007, where I used flowers and materials that are often shared in family situations or communal events. At funerals, for example.

We all have experiences with flowers–receiving them, giving them, or even just seeing them in different states, whether they're blooming or decaying. And I like the openness of that. Using them is also a poetic gesture. I wanted to incorporate the flower petals as a way to think about this maintenance of commemoration and also about how you tend to something. That gesture is something temporal or ephemeral, but for me it's also activated by a body, by an actual person. I like that relationship.

But I came to the use of materials like the flower petals out of a real sense of anxiety I have about life and death–this was my way of attaching it to a gesture that allows me to think about creating something. I'm thinking about other artists, like Félix González-Torres or Ana Mendieta, for instance, who were using these everyday materials but were also thinking about how their work related to larger questions about life.

KR: You consulted the holdings of the Field Museum in Chicago, and one of their Chimú pots ended up being the source material for one of your sculptures. Can you speak about your interest in pre-Columbian sculptures and the life of such objects?

HM: I think my question is really about the agency embedded in these artifacts. There's a power. There's history in the way that they represent a particular place and time, but they're housed by these museums, where objects are in a continual state of stasis. But these objects are already imbued with life, and there's this specter of history attached to them. There's obviously a trace of the history of colonialism and the exploitation of resources from the Americas.

KR: I would also love to hear more about your decision to make a 3-D copy as a way to transform the pot.

HM: I knew that I wouldn't be able to use the actual object in the way that I would have liked to, but I thought that maybe a process of transformation could help bridge its past and its present. The Field Museum—well, museums in general, I think, are trying to prevent the death of these objects or their decay. Candice Hopkins (see pages 11-15) and I were discussing this and asking, "Well, how do we engage with those things?" Because of the way the pot was collected, we don't know much about its original use, but it likely held either a funerary or a ceremonial function. And it had a relationship to the body.

Museums like the Field are doing 3-D scans of their collections and allowing artists and scholars to think about them and reinterpret them and maybe have a different engagement with them. I thought maybe this would be a good opportunity to see where that could go. So it's in line with these things that I'm thinking about—the body, fragmentation, these vessels. I placed a speaker inside of the pot so that the voice from the sound installation would activate it and reanimate it. I kept thinking about this idea of transformation. For me, it opened up a lot of opportunities, as well as a lot of concerns and questions about how to work with these objects, and if they're being remade or given new functions and narratives. And I think that more and more, there are lots of artists from my generation who are looking at and wanting to engage with this material historically, and bring it into a more contemporary moment.

KR: Both your sculptural installation *The years now* and the photograph *Consent not to be a single being,* also included in the exhibition, suggest a site the viewer is encountering after an event has occurred. Could you talk about the indexical nature of both your photographs and your sculptures?

HM: With that photo in particular—or even with the use of the flower petals—there is a suggestion of an event that's already passed. In terms of the index there are these encounters—what you're looking at in the image are the leftovers or detritus that is left behind by the living for the dead. All you really see are the traces or residue. And it took me a long time to make that connection, to think about the index in that way.

I see a connection between *Consent not to be a single being* and *Elmina Castle,* a photograph I took while studying in Ghana of one of the major trading posts of the Atlantic slave trade. In each image there's an evocation of the body. In one of the pictures you see the fresh traces of blood on a ground, and in the other one there's a shadow overlooking a marked-up floor that has this accumulation of blood on its surface. They also share the same perspective, placing the viewer in relation to the site and scale of each location. If you look at them formally, they're somewhat similar. And although they're not easily identifiable, they imply a narrative about each place. They're pictures that ask for a closer view. They're both about looking at very specific sites, but geographically you have these two locations—Havana, Cuba, and Ghana, in West Africa—that have their own historical relationships to one another but are also quite different. And there's a long span of time between when these images were taken and when I knew what to do with them. The events that happened in these places are very, very different and I was not a witness to either. But by being there, I am witness to these sites. Whether or not it's a site or an object that you're encountering, the objects in these photographs are stand-ins for the body in some way, similar to the way that I'm discussing the use of the flower petals as being representative of a body. These are objects that are often found at these sites and are to be used later on.

KR: *The years now* references multiple sites and histories. How do you think about bringing these sites, places, and time periods together in your work?

HM: I think that is tied to my upbringing. Geographically, thinking about the dynamics of a place like Medellín, Colombia, or Zacatecas, Mexico–they're very different locations physically and culturally. And then there is Chicago, of course. So those three places, I would say, have been very instrumental in terms of how my identity was shaped and how I think about representation. What I want to do is think about a crisscross between places that reference multiple histories that are still present. Colombia, Cuba, or Ghana, for instance. There's also this connection between your sense of self and where your family is from. For me, that's not solely in the past. That's still very much present, and it's still something I continue to engage with.

There are other places that I've visited that have also allowed me to consider this broader constellation and the connection between both place and self. And so what happens is that there are all these fragments now, where I'm either taking photographs here or I'm collecting materials there or I'm researching histories, etc.

Later on I assemble these things from different places and different ways of working. And then these things get stitched together, when I'm able to have a clearer narrative about a body of work or an exhibition. I think in some ways it mirrors the way that I've been raised or the way that I am as a person in the world. So it has to do with history, and then it also has to do with the very current present. And none of that is ever linear.

KR: Can you elaborate on what role the element of time plays in your work?

HM: I try to strive for work that is contemplative or that allows you to engage with it in a slower manner. I know that that's not always possible. But in terms of images, for instance, I'm always trying to slow down the reading or the consumption of that image. In some work, it reads clearly as an image from a distance, but when you get close to it you realize that there's all this materiality on the surface–like a skin or creases–that you're now looking at, and it's not just this flat surface. And I think there's definitely time that's embedded in all of the sculptures. *but I sound better since you cut my throat* is a very good example of time–before and after–there's a real inherent violence or growth or transformation or transmutation in that object. It still has this agency even if it's removed from its source as a body or a being.

In my photographs and sculptures there is a sense of change happening but it's slow. And the work is quiet in that sense. The change happens very gradually and I'm okay with that. That's something that I've really thought about. There's something that's getting exposed, something that is slowly changing over a period of time.

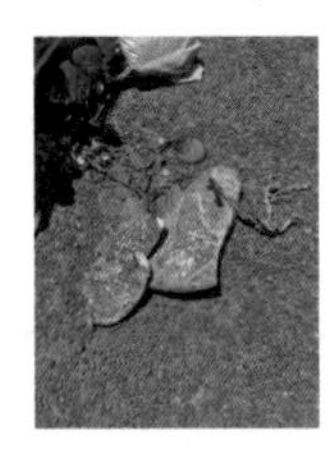

Cochineal, San Juan Teotihuacán, Mexico, 2018

El Astillero, Zacatecas, Mexico, 2018

when the night is going wrong or when the day is full of empty promise, 2017. Handcrafted sterling silver with iridescent applied patina and water (continuously replenished). Collaboration with Tiffany & Co. for the 2017 Whitney Biennial, Whitney Museum of American Art, New York. Courtesy the artist, Tiffany & Co., and the Whitney Museum of American Art, New York

Study for *when the night is going wrong or when the day is full of empty promise*, 2017. Toner on paper

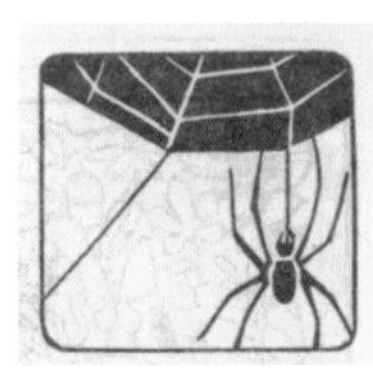

"Al Acecho," from *Historia Natural, Album De Chocolatina Jet*, 1967. Illustrations by Serra Aya, Dionisio Nadal, and Jorge Nuñez

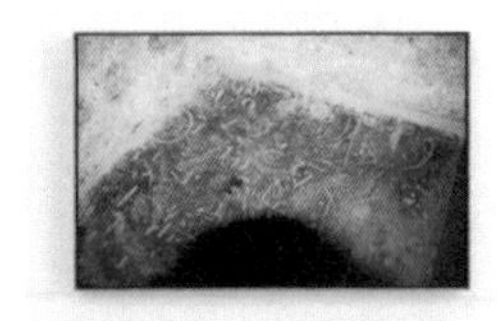

Elmina Castle, 2016. Archival pigment print transferred from color slide film shot in 1999, mounted on Dibond, with unique bronze artist's frame. Photo: Aron Gent

Margarita, 2016. Reclaimed foam from a baseball batting helmet; broken glass; dried foliage; owl, rooster, and vulture feathers from El Astillero, Zacatecas, Mexico; and steel. Private collection, Chicago. Photo: Aron Gent, courtesy the artist and PATRON Gallery, Chicago

Margarita, 2016. Reclaimed foam from a baseball batting helmet; broken glass; dried foliage; owl, rooster, and vulture feathers from El Astillero, Zacatecas, Mexico; and steel. Private collection, Chicago. Photo: Aron Gent, courtesy the artist and PATRON Gallery, Chicago

I did not become someone different / That I did not want to be (detail), 2016. Reclaimed wrought iron, steel, dead staghorn fern, moss, coconut, and lemon-lime Kool-Aid. Private collection. Photo: Aron Gent, courtesy the artist and PATRON Gallery, Chicago

Folio 24: "Tribute owed every eighty days by the towns of the Zapotec region of Coyolapan in the central part of Oaxaca, including twenty bags of cochineal," from *Matrícula de tributes: Nuevos estudios* (early 16th century). Biblioteca Nacional de Antropología y Historia, Mexico City

Folio 23: "Annual tribute owed by the towns in Coaixtlahuacan region in the northern part of the state of Oaxaca to the Aztec Empire, including forty bags of *grana cochinilla* (indicated by two red-spotted bags), equivalent to two *zurrónes*, or Spanish leather sacks," from *Matrícula de tributos: Nuevos estudios* (early 16th century). Biblioteca Nacional de Antropología y Historia, Mexico City

II

But I sound better since you cut my throat, 2017.

Reclaimed galvanized steel, wood, and chain link fence

HAROLD MENDEZ

HAROLD MENDEZ

Untitled, 2012.
Resin-coated photo paper

Street vendor, Chicago, 2006.
Partially exposed color slide film

Bosque de Chapultepec,
Mexico City, 2016

El Astillero, Zacatecas, Mexico, 2018

Study for *Siempre serás*, 2017.
Archival pigment print

Untitled, 2018–20. Obsidian and water
(continuously replenished)

Judge (1), 2016–17. Resin-coated photo
paper, silkscreen ink, and paper pulp

Excavation in Machu Picchu, Peru, 2015

Domingo (detail), 2019. Sand paper; animal
fat; pigment; and owl, rooster, and vulture
feathers backed with fiberglass mesh.
Photo: Aron Gent

José Antonio de Alzate y Ramírez,
illustration of a cochineal collection, 1777.
Newberry Library, Chicago, Edward E. Ayer
Manuscript Collection

Street vendor, Chicago, 2006.
Color slide film

Study for *The night of counting the years
(Offering)* (detail), 2019. Five-plate
lithograph

III
Installation view of *Harold Mendez: The years now*,
Reva and David Logan Center for the Arts
at the University of Chicago, 2020

HAROLD MENDEZ

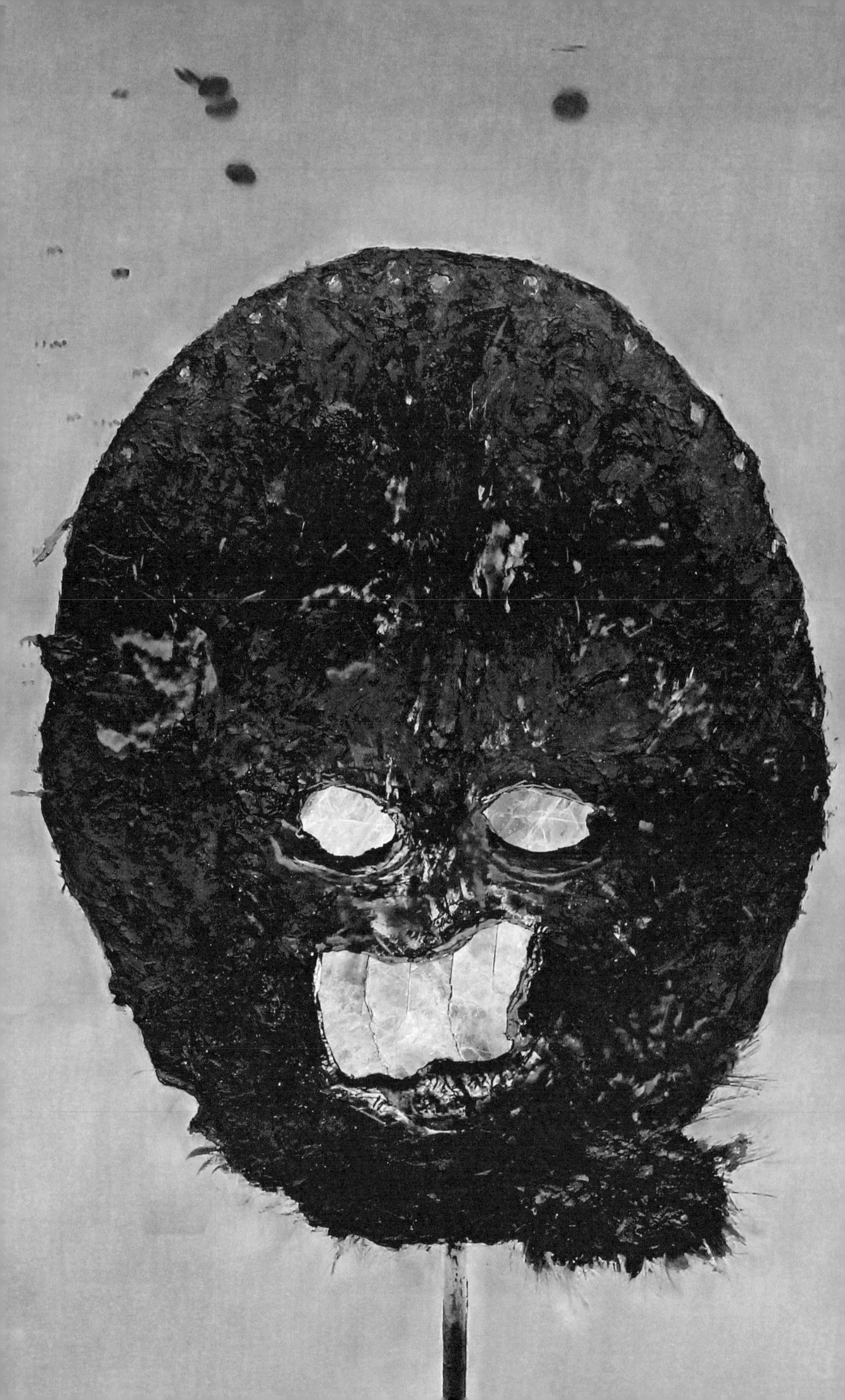

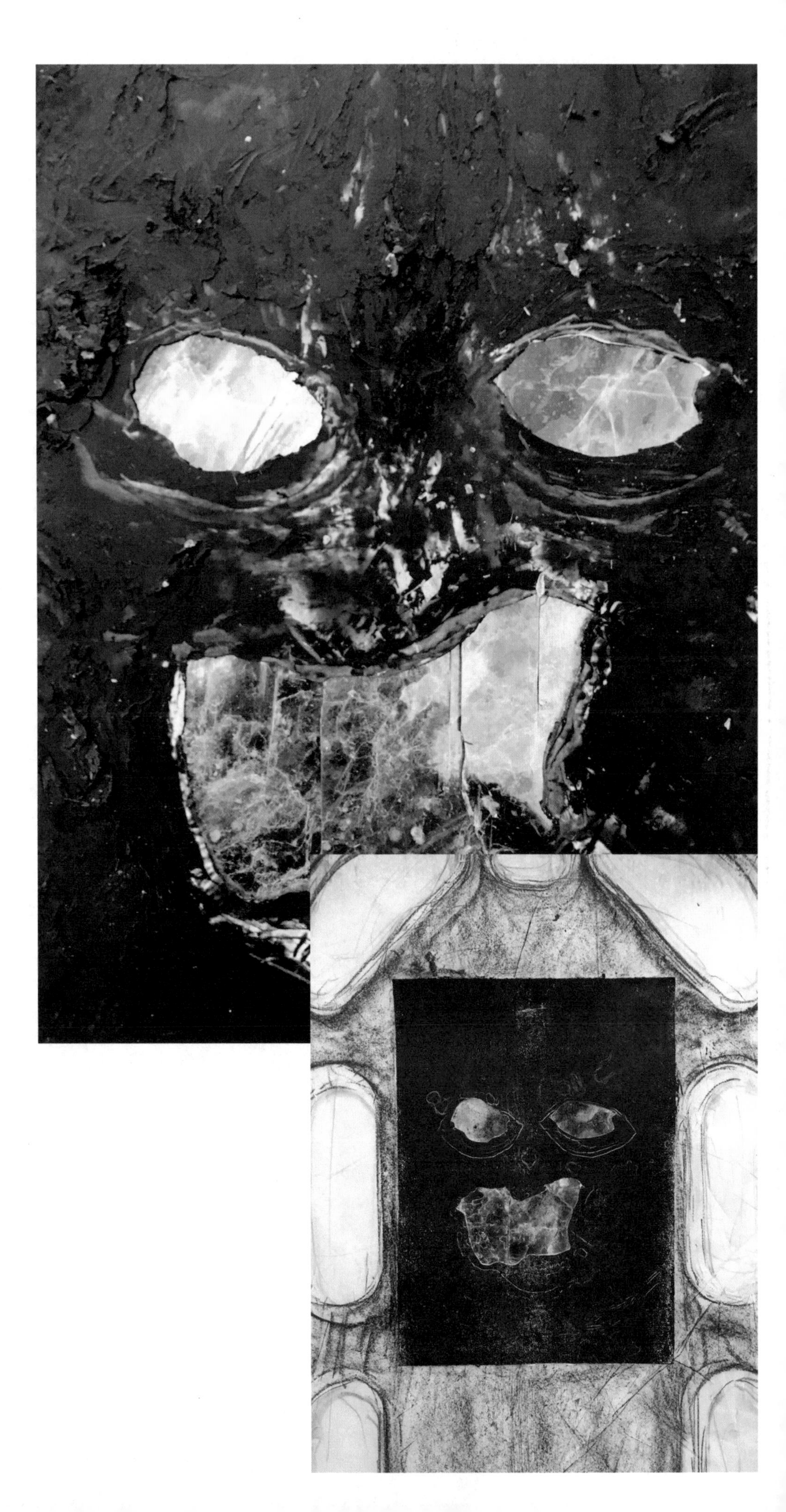

HAROLD MENDEZ

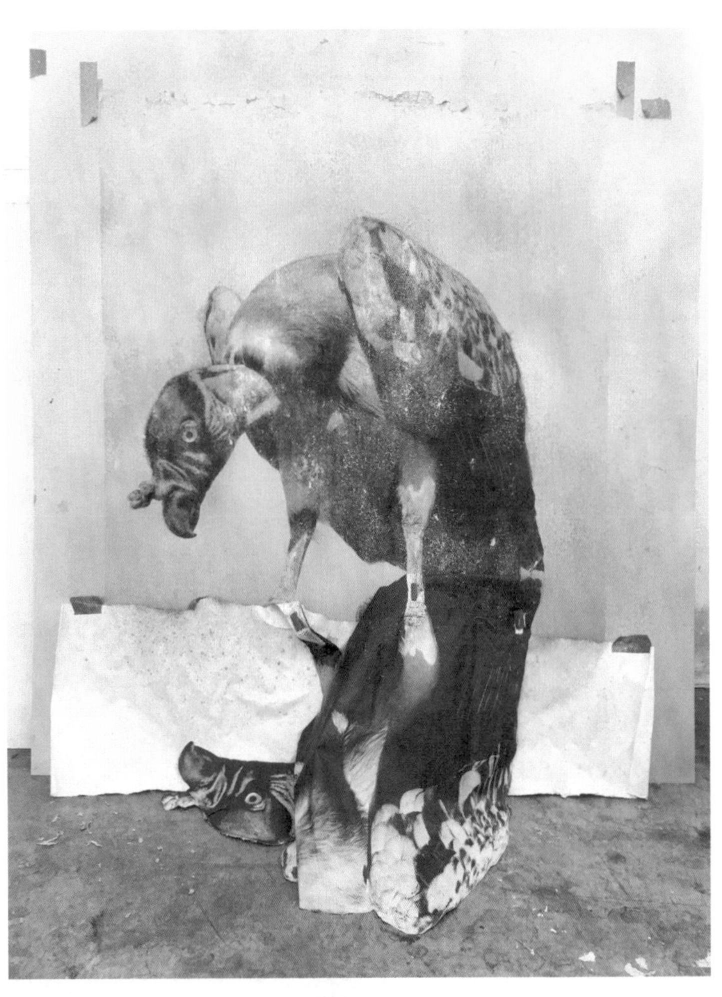

HAROLD MENDEZ

Elmina Castle, Ghana, 1999

Untitled (Mask) (detail), 2019.
Archival pigment print, oil stick, and graphite

Mask (detail), 2019. Archival pigment print, oil stick, graphite, mica, and collage on paper. The Berger Family Collection. Photo: Daniel Hojnacki, courtesy the artist and PATRON Gallery, Chicago

Túpac Amaru I, ca. 1850–70.
Museo Nacional de Arqueología, Antropología e Historia del Perú, Lima

Mama Huaco, 1616. The J. Paul Getty Museum, Los Angeles, Ms. Ludwig XIII 16, fol. 23

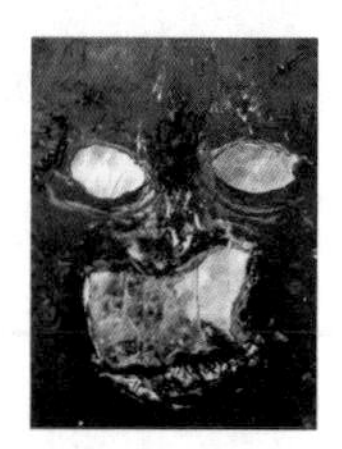

Mask (detail), 2019. Archival pigment print, oil stick, graphite, mica, and collage on paper. The Berger Family Collection. Photo: Daniel Hojnacki, courtesy the artist and PATRON Gallery, Chicago

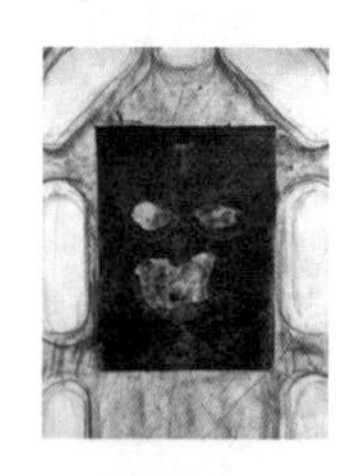

Study (Untitled) (detail), 2019.
Lithographic crayon, toner, indigo, graphite, mica, and collage on paper

Still from *In Necuepaliztli in Aztlan* (Return to Aztlán), dir. Juan Mora Catlett, 1990. © 1990, 2012, JUAN ROBERTO MORA CATLETT D.R.

Javelina, El Astillero, Zacatecas, Mexico, 2018

Studio view of *Wake*, 2019. Cotton, spray enamel, metallic paint, toner, graphite, watercolor, and lithographic crayon on ball-grained aluminum lithographic plate mounted on Dibond

Busto de Gaitàn destruido, 2014.
Biblioteca Pública Piloto de Medellín para América Latina

Study for *let X stand, if it can for the one's unfound (After Proceso Pentágono)*, 2016.
Collage, toner, and graphite on paper

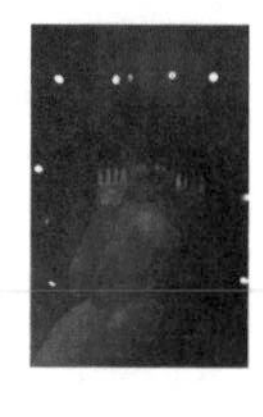

Maritime Peoples of the Arctic and Pacific Northwest Coast, Wooden Totem Pole, Field Museum of Natural History, Chicago, 2019–20

Skowhegan, Maine, 2013

Figura 285: "Strychnos rondeletoides Sprice. *N. v. Curare,*" from *El Herbario Nacional Colombiano*. Medellín, Colombia, 2018

Manco Capac, 1616. The J. Paul Getty Museum, Los Angeles, Ms. Ludwig XIII 16, fol. 21

IV

Consent not to be a single being, 2018.

Archival pigment print mounted on Dibond

HAROLD MENDEZ

NO CONDITION IS PERMANENT

THE YEARS NOW

logique Réutilisab
s dans la nature

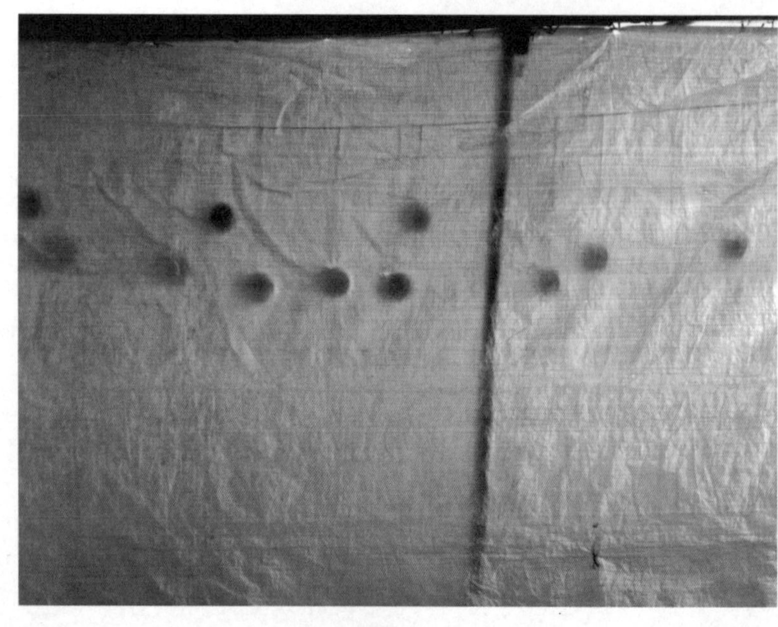

Los Angeles, 2018

Aguas Calientes, Peru, 2015

Volta Region, Ghana, 1999

San Juan Teotihuacán, Mexico, 2018

Vejigante, Chicago, ca. 2000

Aguas Calientes, Peru, 2015

Collection of stones, El Astillero, Zacatecas, Mexico, 2018

Salt lick, El Astillero, Zacatecas, Mexico, 2018

Mica mine, Ojo Caliente, New Mexico, 2014

Medellín, Colombia, 2014

Study for *At the edge of the Necrópolis*, Havana, 2017–18

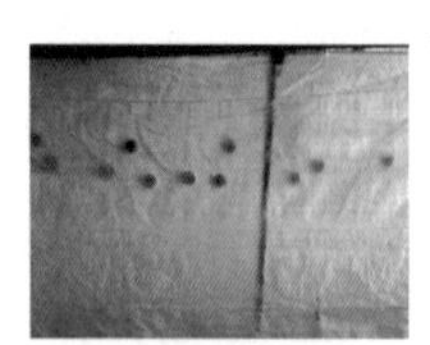

Cuzco, Peru, 2015

Selecting obsidian, San Juan Teotihuacán, Mexico, 2018

Selecting obsidian (detail), San Juan Teotihuacán, Mexico, 2018

Fragment of a quiver, Middle Kingdom, Dynasty 11, ca. 2124–1981 B.C.E. The Metropolitan Museum of Art, New York, Rogers Fund, 1928

Textile fragment with stripes and confronted birds, ca. 475–221 B.C.E. The Metropolitan Museum of Art, New York, purchase, The Vincent Astor Foundation Gift, 2002

V

The years now (transcript), 2019–20.
Collage, graphite, and toner on paper

more painful

more often

more crying out upside down… dangling… sadly (*reverb*)

who am I?

WHO AM I?

the louder I ask, the louder becomes a silence of no answer until it seems that silence is saying (*reverb*)

by saying nothing–you ain't nothing

but to somebody i AM

somewhere within - yet unknown

rebels at the very question: do not ask who am I

you will know what needs to be known when you ask instead

whose am I?

where shall I go?…..

and from the pain of life’s first blow

came the joy of life’s first breath

cried out

upside down

dangling

    happily

I AM!

I aAmmM *(reverb)*

the years now…

harder blows

more painful

THE YEARS NOW

KARMA
IS a
MUTHa

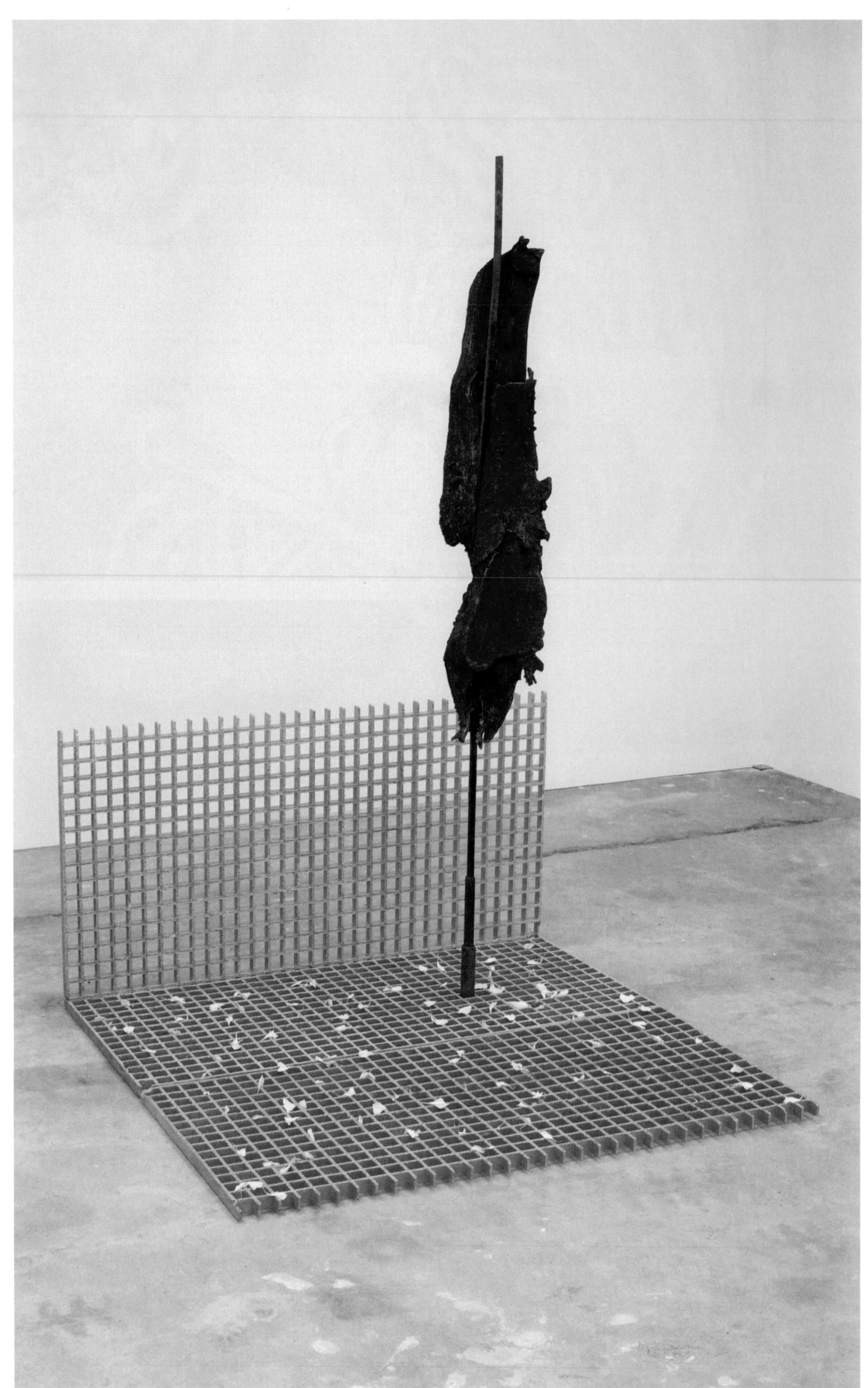

Ejido el Tejuján, Zacatecas, Mexico, 2018

Aguas Calientes, Peru, 2015.
Photo: Argenis Apolinario, courtesy
Argenis Apolinario and Harold Mendez

Aguas Calientes, Peru, 2015

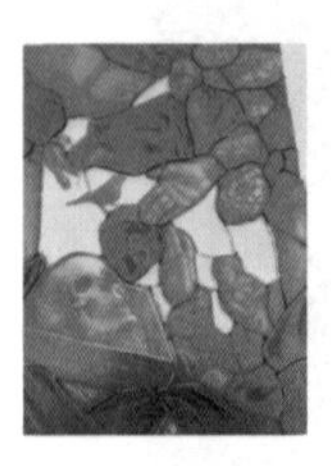

Stained glass produced by Franz Mayer
of Munich, Inc., Munich, Germany, 2013

Aguas Calientes, Peru, 2015.
Photo: Argenis Apolinario, courtesy
Argenis Apolinario and Harold Mendez

Aguas Calientes, Peru, 2015.
Photo: Argenis Apolinario, courtesy
Argenis Apolinario and Harold Mendez

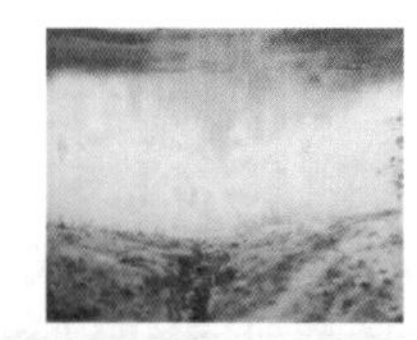

Installation view of *Panic dwindled into jitters into detached fascination./ It was just a show. The longer I watched the less I felt./ Events coupled, cavorted, and vanished, emotion hanging in mid air/ before my lemur eyes like a thin shred of homeless ectoplasm./ It was cool. It was like drowning in syrup,* 2008–11. Black silicon carbide, industrial ink, natural dyes (alloe mossey bay extract, cochineal, cutch extract, logwood extract, osage orange sawdust), various mordents, and marking beads on canvas. Collection of Darryl Atwell

Third Ward, Houston, 2013

Anzá, Colombia, 2014

Adinkra stamps (detail).
Kumasi, Ghana, 1999

Adinkra stamps,
Kumasi, Ghana, 1999

American Pictures, 2017.
Reclaimed wrought iron, wood, crushed cochineal insects, staples, fiberglass, and carnations (continuously replenished).
Private collection

Installation view of *I'm not always fitting (After Koudelka),* 2014/2020.
Reclaimed glass, bricks, and soot.
Photo: Jeff McLane, courtesy the Institute of Contemporary Art, Los Angeles

Polish cochineal insects, 1764.
Illustration by James Mynde.
©The Royal Society

Shozo Kadai's *Form 12* (1958), 2017

VI
The years now (detail), 2020.
Fiberglass, carnation petals (continuously replenished), spray enamel, speakers, transducer, amplifier, wood, steel, charcoal, graphite, 3-D printed sculpture, and multichannel sound installation

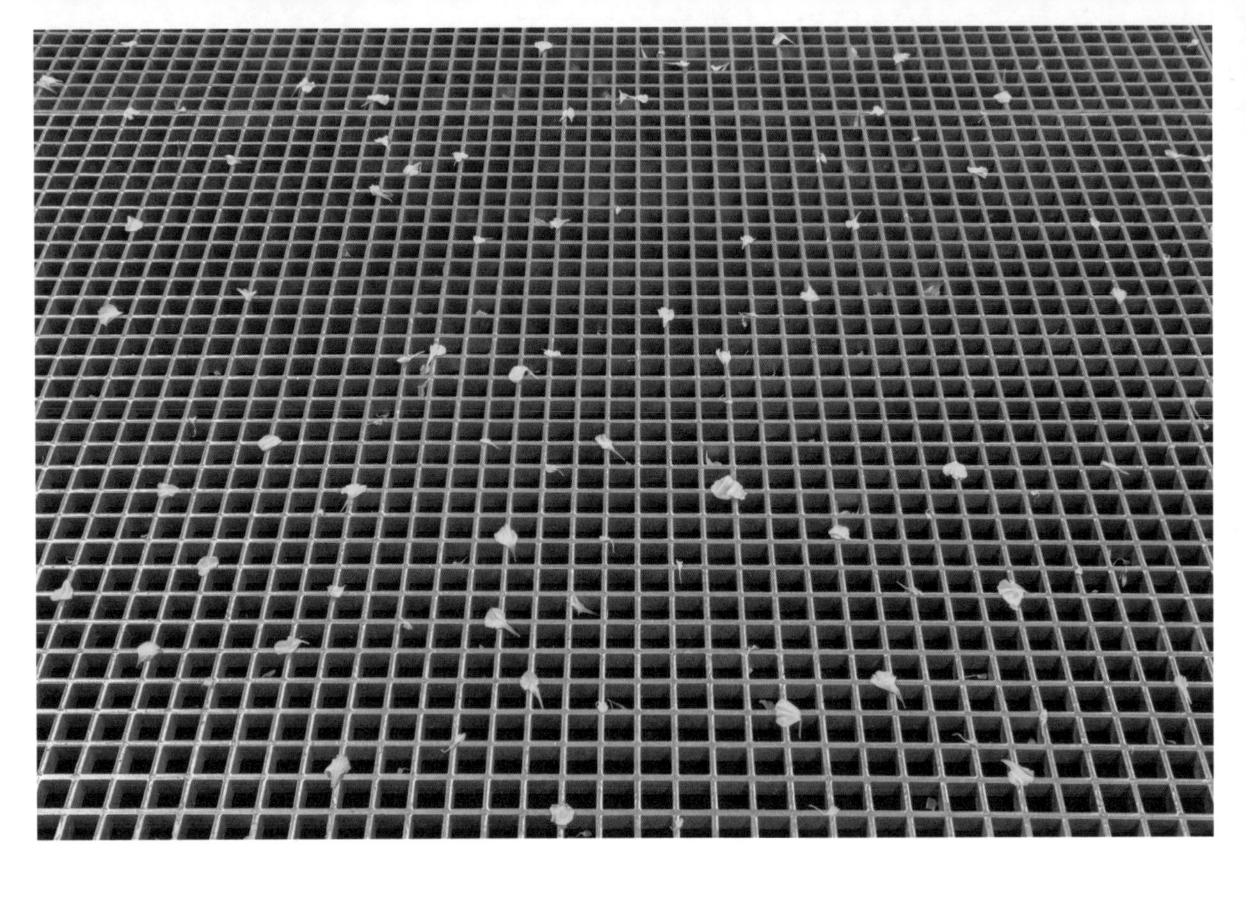

AM

PIC

ICAN

URES

Luxor, Egypt, 2010

El Templete, Havana, 2017-20

Had the price of looking been blindness, I would have looked (For Ralph Ellison), 2014. Paper, tri-directional foil, fiberglass, synthetic rubber, toner, watercolor, spray enamel graphite, oil crayon, and soot mounted on Dibond, 37 x 50 in. (94 x 127 cm). Green / Beneck Collection. Photo: Argenis Apolinario

Luxor, Egypt, 2010

Luxor, Egypt, 2010

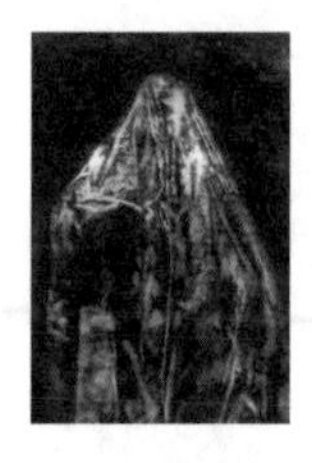

I'm not always fitting (After Koudelka) (detail), 2014. Reclaimed glass, bricks, and soot

Museo Anahuacalli, Tepetlapa, Coyoacán, Mexico, 2019

Chapala, Jalisco, Mexico, 2019

American Pictures, 2018. Collage, ink, and graphite on paper

American Pictures, 2018. Collage, ink, and graphite on paper

Study for *And why not also in the self, the odd blocks, all lost and left,* 2010–14. Collage, ink, graphite on paper

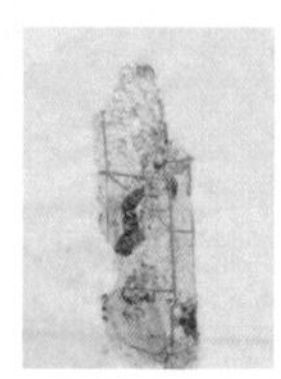

And why not also in the self, the odd blocks, all lost and left (detail), 2010–14. Mixed-media on tracing paper, vellum, graphite, colored pencil, aluminum foil from my mother's kitchen stove gas burners, food matter, vegetable oil, and transparent spray enamel. Collection of Leslie and Brad Bucher

Study for *And why not also in the self, the odd blocks, all lost and left,* 2010–14. Collage, ink, and graphite on paper

Afterwards, we shall read your bones (For Belkis Ayón) (detail), 2019. Archival pigment print, collage, and telson (Horseshoe crab) on paper. Private collection, promised gift on long-term loan to Minneapolis Institute of Art. Photo by: Aron Gent, courtesy the artist and PATRON Gallery, Chicago

Figure 1: "*Porphyrophora hamelii* (Armenian cochineal)," in *Naturhistorische Bemerkungen über Wurzelcochenille im Vergleich zur mexicanischen* (1833)

Chimú tunic, 12th-15th century. The Metropolitan Museum of Art, New York, the Michael C. Rockefeller Memorial Collection, bequest of Nelson A. Rockefeller, 1979

VII

The years now (detail), 2020.
Fiberglass, carnation petals (continuously replenished),
spray enamel, speakers, transducer, amplifier, wood,
steel, charcoal, graphite, 3-D printed sculpture,
and multichannel sound installation

Contenido

Jacob Holdt, *Flowers on SF Beach,* from *American Pictures* (1977). © Jacob Holdt

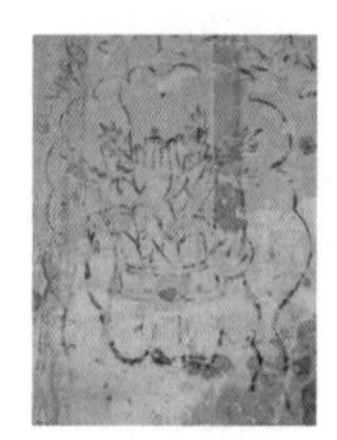

Valparaíso, Zacatecas, Mexico, 2018

Regla, Havana, 2017

The night of counting the years (detail), 2019. Pigmented print, graphite, watercolor, colored pencil, and fiberglass screen. Collection of Susan Berkowitz and Bob Higgins. Photo: Aron Gent, courtesy the artist and PATRON Gallery, Chicago

Figure 54: "Cecropia aff. arachnoides Pittier. N. v. *Yarumo,*" from *El Herbario Nacional Colombiano.* Medellín, Colombia, 2018

"Migala Albañil," from *Historia Natural, Album De Chocolatina Jet* (1967). Illustrations by Serra Aya, Dionisio Nadal, and Jorge Nuñez

La Necrópolis de Cristóbal Colón, Havana, 2017

El Astillero, Zacatecas, Mexico, 2018

New Mexico, 2014

Peyote, El Astillero, Zacatecas, Mexico, 2018

Anzá, Colombia, 2014

El Astillero, Zacatecas, Mexico, 2018

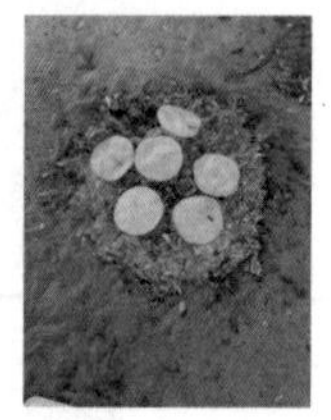

Ejido el Tejuján, Zacatecas, Mexico, 2018

Anzá, Colombia, 2014

Ejido el Tejuján, Zacatecas, Mexico, 2018

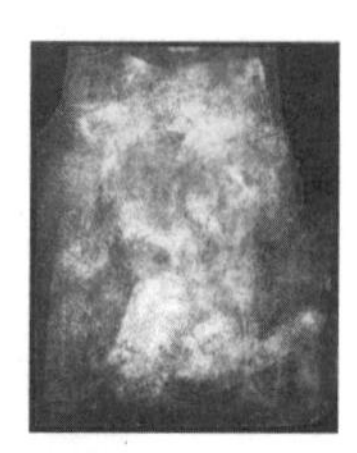

Antioquia (II), 2016. Unique silkscreen on linen

"Tarántula," from *Historia Natural, Album De Chocolatina Jet* (1967). Illustrations by Serra Aya, Dionisio Nadal, and Jorge Nuñez

VIII

The years now (detail), 2020.
Fiberglass, carnation petals (continuously replenished),
spray enamel, speakers, transducer, amplifier, wood,
steel, charcoal, graphite, 3-D printed sculpture,
and multichannel sound installation

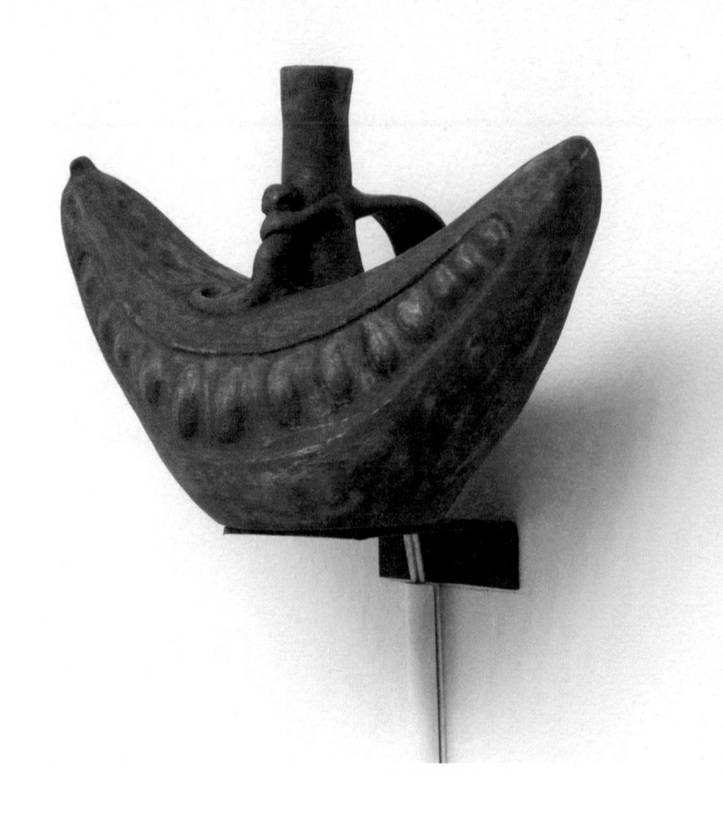

HAROLD MENDEZ

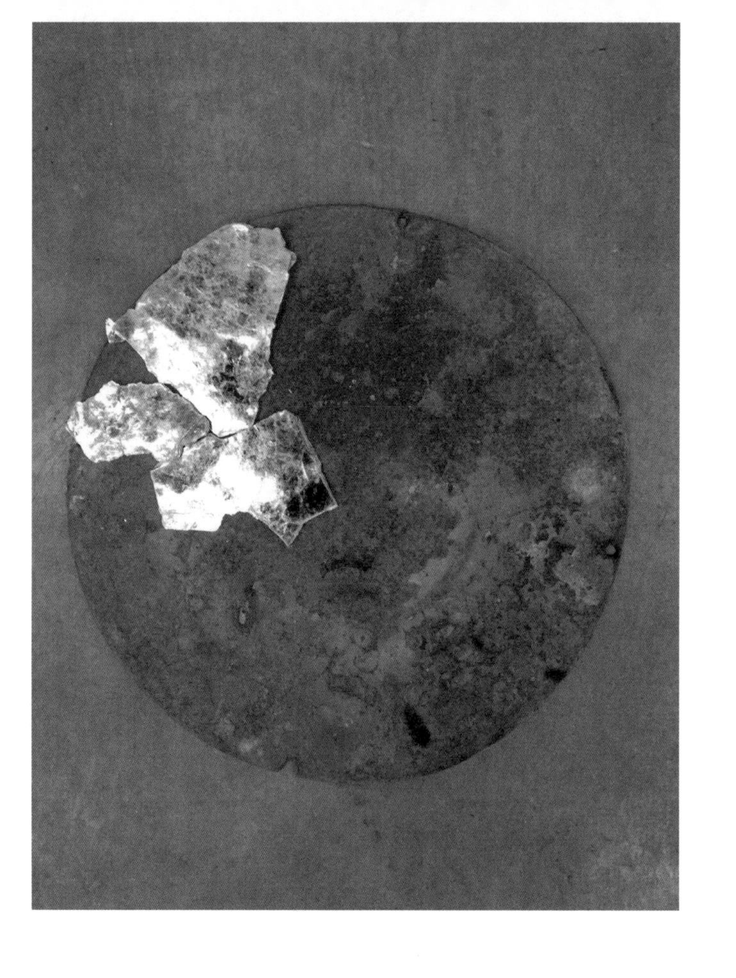

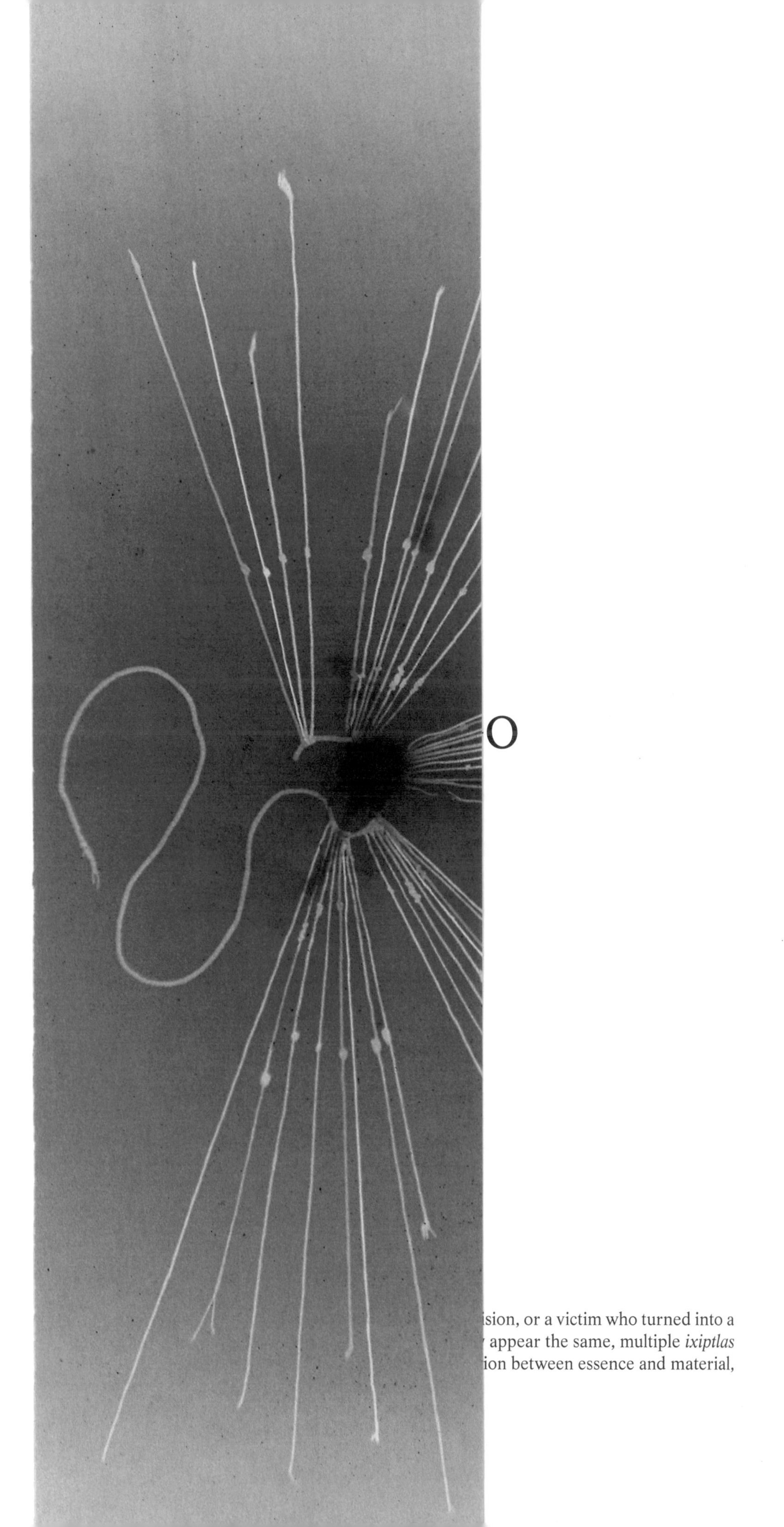

O

ision, or a victim who turned into a
appear the same, multiple *ixiptlas*
ion between essence and material,

We the pedestal, the spear sung the animal fat
to feather, image delegate sheared from flesh,
now sounding the lantern, the veils through
the veils.

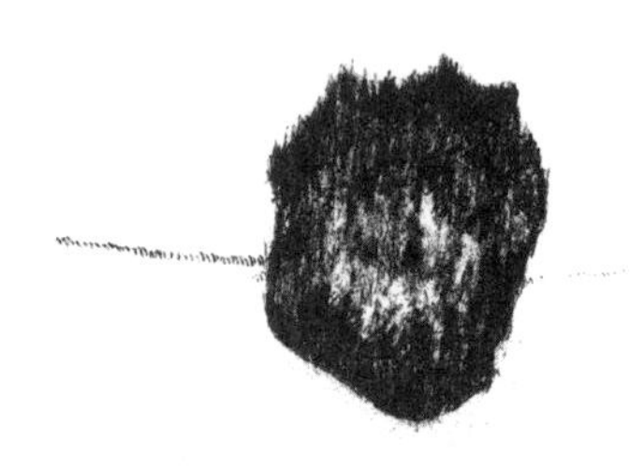

You shattered to me a sky

given to sound, the

human  the bells

shattered; as an eyeless black shears between essence & material between original & copy: the flesh, & the flesh, & the flesh.

We children of lanterns culled we
must fracture the fiber the tendon & bone;
we children charnel-sung moved by love, the
world many love moved,

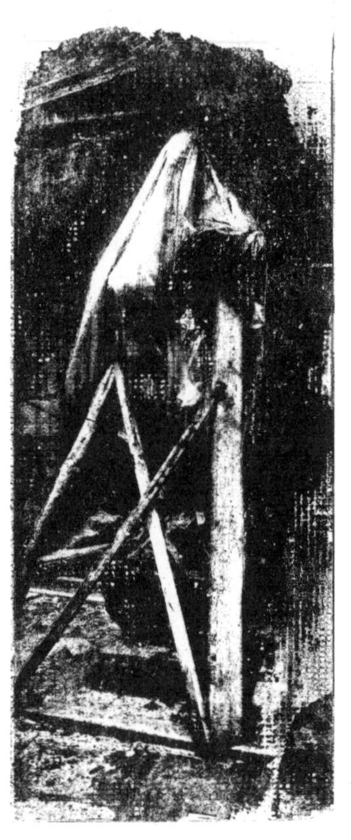

beseech: if we are meat & nerve,
we children femur fractured talon-song, angel-
stretched, & born of rabid gardens–Listen
as if the heart were the most promised hymn.

HAROLD MENDEZ

And, perhaps, here, between, our deaths sing *us*: faces sheared, facing the other shore, the name outside

under our eyes with gold, a separate love

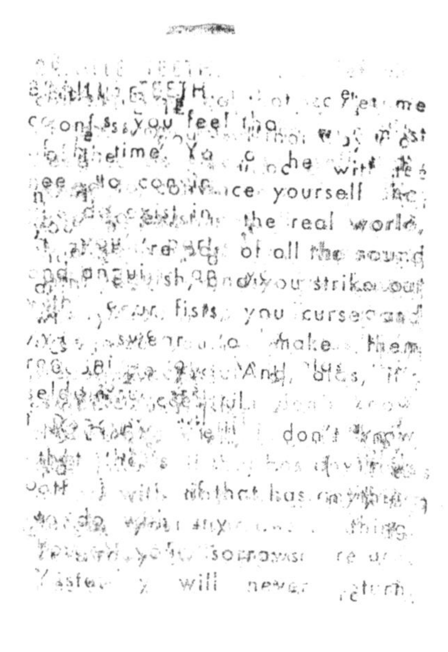

sounding  the

same god simultaneous,

the further sun

born of

parallel light.

Untitled (X), 2016.
Photo chemicals on paper

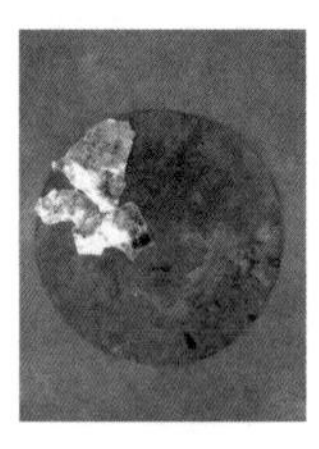

Studio view, Houston, 2005-6.
Mica on cardboard

Third Ward, Houston, 2016

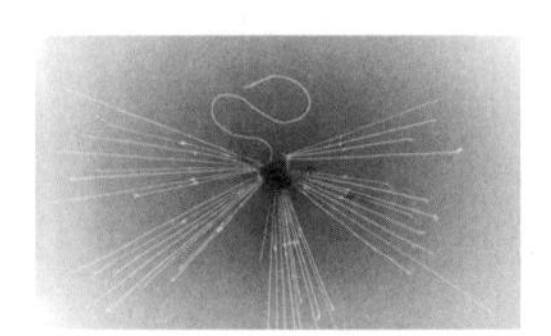

Quipu, Field Museum of Natural History,
Chicago, 2019-20

Cape Coast Castle, Ghana, 1999

Arican tunic, 15th-early 16th century.
The Metropolitan Museum of Art, New York,
gift of John B. Elliott through the Mercer
Trust, 2000

Incan tunic, 15th-early 16th century.
The Metropolitan Museum of Art,
New York, Rogers Fund, 1982

IX

The years now (detail), 2020.
Fiberglass, carnation petals (continuously replenished),
spray enamel, speakers, transducer, amplifier, wood,
steel, charcoal, graphite, 3-D printed sculpture,
and multichannel sound installation

Candice Hopkins

Candice Hopkins works as senior curator for the Toronto Biennial of Art. She previously served as co-curator of the 2018 SITE Santa Fe biennial, *Casa Tomada*; and as part of the curatorial team for Documenta 14 in Athens and Kassel, Germany. She also co-curated the major exhibitions *Sakahàn: International Indigenous Art,* National Gallery of Canada, Ottawa; *Close Encounters: The Next 500 Years*, various venues; and the 2014 SITElines biennial, *Unsettled Landscapes,* Santa Fe. Her writing has been published widely; recent essays and presentations include "Outlawed Social Life" for *South as a State of Mind* magazine and *Sounding the Margins: A Choir of Minor Voices,* Small Projects, Tromsø, Norway. She has lectured internationally, including at the Witte de With Center for Contemporary Art, Tate Modern, Dak'Art: African Contemporary Art Biennale, Artists Space, Tate Britain, and the University of British Columbia. She is the recipient of numerous awards, including the Hnatyshyn Foundation Visual Arts Award for Curatorial Excellence in Contemporary Art and the Foundation Prince Pierre de Monaco's 2016 Prix pour un essai critique sur l'art contemporain. She is a citizen of the Carcross/Tagish First Nation.

J. Michael Martinez

J. Michael Martinez is the author of three collections of poetry. Long-listed for the National Book Award, he is a winner of the National Poetry Series and a recipient of the Walt Whitman Award from the Academy of American Poets. He has published with various outlets, including PBS, The Poetry Society of America's New American Poets series, *New American Writing,* and *POETRY* magazine. He is the poetry editor at Noemi Press and his writings have been anthologized in Ahsahta Press' The Arcadia Project: North American Postmodern Pastoral, Rescue Press' The New Census: 40 American Poets, and Counterpath Press' Angels of the Americlypse: New Latin@ Writing. A visiting assistant professor of poetry at St. Lawrence University, Canton, Martinez lives in upstate New York.

Harold Mendez

Harold Mendez has taken part in significant exhibitions, including *Being: New Photography,* the Museum of Modern Art, New York, and the 2017 Whitney Biennial, New York. In addition, his work has been the subject of exhibitions at the Institute of Contemporary Art, Los Angeles; the Studio Museum in Harlem; the Bass Museum, Miami; LAXART, Los Angeles; the Institute of Contemporary Art, Philadelphia; MoMA PS1, New York; the Renaissance Society, Chicago; Project Row Houses, Houston; and the Museum of Contemporary Art, Chicago, among other venues. He has been an artist-in-residence at the Robert Rauschenberg Foundation; Core Program, Museum of Fine Arts, Houston; Skowhegan School of Painting and Sculpture; Headlands Center for the Arts; Light Work; and the Arts/Industry program, John Michael Kohler Arts Center. His works are included in the permanent collections of the Whitney Museum of American Art, New York; Studio Museum in Harlem; the Museum of Fine Arts, Houston; the J.P. Morgan Chase Art Collection; Minneapolis Institute of Art; DePaul Art Museum, Chicago; and the Colección Diéresis, Guadalajara, Mexico. Mendez studied at Columbia College Chicago; the University of Science and Technology, School of Art, Ghana; and the University of Illinois at Chicago. He is currently based in Los Angeles.

Katja Rivera

Katja Rivera was formerly assistant curator, Logan Center Exhibitions at the Reva and David Logan Center for the Arts, University of Chicago, where she curated the exhibition *Harold Mendez: The years now*. Her recent curatorial projects include *Traduttore, Traditore* (Gallery 400, University of Illinois at Chicago), which explored translation beyond its linguistic meaning in contemporary practices. Rivera has worked in curatorial departments at the Eli and Edythe Broad Art Museum, Michigan State University, and at the Art Institute of Chicago, where she helped organize the first U.S. solo presentation of the Brazilian artist Tarsila do Amaral. Rivera holds an MA in art history from the University of Texas at Austin and is currently a PhD candidate at the University of Illinois at Chicago. She specializes in modern and contemporary art with a focus on experimental practices in Mexico.

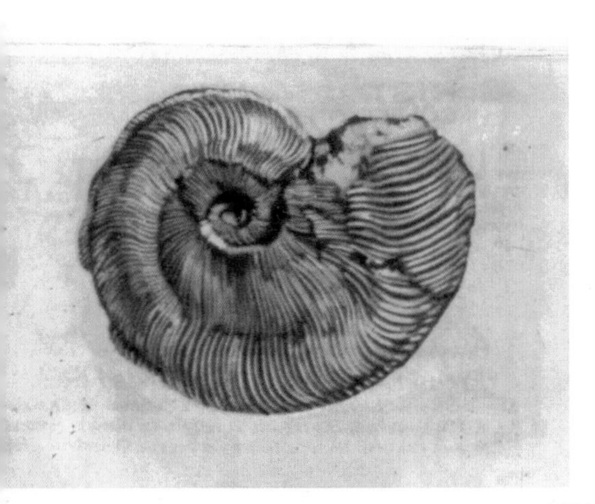

Studio view of *Sin nombre* in progress for the exhibition *New Photography,* The Museum of Modern Art, New York, 2018

Studio view, Los Angeles, 2017

Untitled, n.d. Glass plate negative. Patrimonio Cultural Oficina del Historiador de la Ciudad, Fototeca Historica, Havana

"Fósiles de la Era Secundaria," from *Historia Natural, Album De Chocolatina Jet* (1967). Illustrations by Serra Aya, Dionisio Nadal, and Jorge Nuñez

Untitled (We are a thousand petals to no one) (detail), 2019. Obsidian, water, and carnations and alstroemeria (continuously replenished). Photo: Daniel Hojnacki

"Eclipse Total De Sol," from *Historia Natural, Album De Chocolatina Jet* (1967). Illustrations by Serra Aya, Dionisio Nadal, and Jorge Nuñez

Havana, 2017

"Astronomia," from *Historia Natural, Album De Chocolatina Jet* (1967). Illustrations by Serra Aya, Dionisio Nadal, and Jorge Nuñez

This publication was produced in conjunction with the exhibition *Harold Mendez: The years now* (January 24–March 8, 2020), curated by Katja Rivera and organized by Logan Center Exhibitions at the Reva and David Logan Center for the Arts at the University of Chicago.

REVA AND DAVID LOGAN CENTER FOR THE ARTS
Executive Director: Bill Michel
Former Director and Curator, Logan Center Exhibitions: Yesomi Umolu
Former Assistant Curator: Katja Rivera
Exhibitions Manager: Alyssa Brubaker
Shop and Gallery Manager: Marcus Warren
Director of Development, UChicago Arts: Stacey Recht
Director of Communications, UChicago Arts and the Logan Center: Ronia Holmes

Major support for *Harold Mendez: The years now* was provided by the David C. and Sarajean Ruttenberg Arts Foundation, The Reva and David Logan Foundation, and friends of the Logan Center.

Generous funding for this publication is provided by the David C. and Sarajean Ruttenberg Arts Foundation and PATRON Gallery, Chicago.

Publication Management: Alyssa Brubaker
Copy Editor and Proofreader: Amanda Glesmann
Exhibition views at the Reva and David Logan Center for the Arts at the University of Chicago photographed by Robert Chase Heishman (pages 19, 31, 43, 79, 91, 103, 115)
Artwork image on page 55 courtesy the artist and PATRON Gallery, Chicago. Photo: Aron Gent

Design: Atelier Letra–Marco Balesteros assisted by Pedro Sousa
Printed by die Keure, Belgium
Cover and end papers: El Astillero, Zacatecas, Mexico, 2018

Library of Congress Control Number: 2020917087
ISBN: 978-0-578-64344-1

Distributed by
The University of Chicago Press
11030 S. Langley Avenue
Chicago, IL 60628 USA
www.press.uchicago.edu